THOSE INVOLVED IN THE CREATION OF THIS

BOOK DEDICATE THE THOUGHTS, PRINCIPLES,

AND LOVE IT CONTAINS TO THE INCREASING

NUMBER OF PEDIATRIC CANCER PATIENTS

WHO HAVE WON THE BATTLE AGAINST THIS

DREADED DISEASE, THOSE YOUNG PEOPLE WHO

ARE CURRENTLY FIGHTING FOR THEIR LIVES,

AND TO THE MEMORY OF THE COURAGEOUS

ANGELS WHO ARE NO LONGER WITH US.

A Championship Heart

What makes a championship heart? What are those special ingredients consistently found in people who excel in life? Certainly, the journey through the human experience is full of challenges, difficulties, hardship and joy – but what makes those select few consistently succeed and rise to the top? Regardless of the endeavor, whether it is sports, business, family, service or in simply living a complete and meaningful life... what is the essence that makes people triumphant?

Two individuals or two teams virtually identical in talent and skills, yet one goes on to become a champion while the other is destined for mediocrity, or the even more gut wrenching position of the perennial runner-up. The almost, but not quite...

What is the "it" that makes such a huge difference? I believe with a certainty founded upon my life's experience, that the "it" is the defining difference between success and failure, between winning and losing... in "living" a life as opposed to simply enduring the passage of a lifetime.

To me "it" is not one thing – rather "it" is a universe of character traits that mature, surround, and ultimately merge within the heart of a champion. In this book, I sought to identify and illustrate the elements of the very unique and special composition that separates the winners from the losers... the things that propel some to go on to succeed when such an outcome does not even seem possible.

With almost a century of winning ways and a history of championships unequaled in professional sports, the Yankees were utilized to convey the traits and characteristics it takes to be a champion on the field and, more importantly, in life. Within that framework, I interviewed numerous players from the Yankees (both past and present), the coaches, the Steinbrenner family, and of course, 'The Boss' himself. Additionally, I had access to hundreds of photographs taken during their championship seasons.

Eighteen key components are highlighted as the core of a championship heart. Few, if any, among us are blessed to have them all. However, the more of these ingredients possessed by the individual, the more likely a champion will be found.

To me, there is no greater championship heart than the one that beats for the betterment of others. It is my fervent hope that this work will be of some value in that pursuit... May all of your dreams and aspirations come true, and each day be filled with the hope of a better tomorrow.

Acknowledgements

This book represents the efforts, dedication, and unwavering commitment of the many people involved in its creation.

First and foremost, I want to thank the Steinbrenner family, the New York Yankees, and members of the organization itself. 'The Boss' was a dear friend with a great heart. He believed in me and the vision of this book. When I first began the project, George granted me full access to him and the Yankees organization. Since that time, his children, Hal, Hank, Jenny and Jessica have done everything asked, and more, in helping me finish it.

I also want to express my deep appreciation to the players, coaches and Manager Joe Girardi for graciously giving their time to me for interviews that resulted in many of the inspirational quotes used in this book.

Many thanks to the great group of former players who met with me and provided further insight into the heart of a champion: the legendary Yogi Berra, Don "Mr. Perfect" Larsen, Reggie "Mr. October" Jackson, Ron "Gator" Guidry, "Goose" Gossage, Mike "Moose" Mussina, good friend Tino Martinez, and my close pal Wade Boggs. As a former pitcher with the Yankees, Richard "Monte" Monteleone, not only provided an interview, he also gave me even more of his time by arranging and accompanying me to meet with several of the retired players and assisted in accessing older Yankees photos. I greatly appreciate the hours spent together, and the friendship we formed. A special thanks to Dave Kaplan of the Yogi Berra Museum, for helping so much with Mr. Berra's interview and showing me around his amazing museum and facilities. It was a great afternoon.

When George passed on, Hal Steinbrenner (Managing General Partner and Co-Chairperson) made certain that the unconditional support and encouragement from the entire Yankees organization continued. I have known Hal since he was a young man, and I have watched his growth and maturity as he has assumed a leadership role with the Yankees, as well as becoming even more of a leader in furthering the Steinbrenner family's legacy of charitable works and giving back to the community. Spending time with Hal on this project was a pleasure and his support was essential. He made the calls, contacts, and put into action whatever was necessary for the book to go forward.

Hank Steinbrenner (General Partner and Co-Chairperson) was also outstanding and very helpful in his contribution. I genuinely enjoyed our discussions about George, Vince Lombardi, and other great leaders. After our lengthy interview, he made a point of going a step further in volunteering his personal time (not just money) to take an active role in helping out at the various events we sponsor for children fighting cancer.

Jenny Steinbrenner has been a friend for many years and she was delightful in sitting with me and recounting stories about her dad. Jenny (General Partner and Vice Chairperson) also was at the center of activity in the development, construction, and transition of the team into the new Yankee Stadium. Her insights into the future of the Yankees concerning continuance of the team's traditions, as well as the kindnesses of her father, were of great benefit.

Jessica Steinbrenner's interview and the morning we spent together was probably the most emotional of all those I did. Jessica (General Partner and Vice Chairperson) is a lover of horses and she is heavily involved in the family's thoroughbred horse operations in Ocala, Florida. She has a big heart and as I got to know her better, it showed. The lessons taught to Jessica by her father were vividly recounted and were invaluable in my efforts to capture the essence of a championship heart. Her husband, Felix Lopez (Chief International Officer and Executive Vice President), participated in our discussions and, subsequently, was kind enough to arrange key interviews for me with some of the players on the Yankees team who came from abroad.

Special thanks to Joan Steinbrenner, George's wife of fifty-four years. As the matriarch of the family, she has always worked "behind the scenes" for the benefit of everyone. When I talked with her about this project, she was kind in giving me encouragement and support.

I particularly want to thank Howard Grosswirth (Vice President of Marketing). Howard is a consummate professional, seems to constantly be in motion, and exemplifies the class and pride of the Yankees organization. His responsibilities involve him with most everything that goes on in Tampa's beautiful Steinbrenner Field. Through the days and weeks that evolved into more than two years, Howard was always there for me and remained committed to this project from its very beginning to its completion. Every step of the way, he worked tirelessly to provide any resources I needed, and became a valued personal friend in the process.

Jason Zillo (Director of Media Relations) went out of his way to give me access to the players and, though I am sure I tried his patience at times, he always came through in accommodating schedules and making the numerous interviews with the players happen. In addition to his official duties, Jason takes the time to get involved in a number of charitable works and gives back. He is a first-class individual.

With a telephone introduction by Hal, I was able to meet Lonn Trost, who is the Chief Operations Officer of the Yankees, and located in New York. Lonn did everything necessary to assure that I was given all the help I needed from the entire organization, and I am appreciative to him.

Through Lonn, I was afforded the opportunity to meet and work with Al Santasiere, III, (Director of Publications). If ever there was an expert in printed materials involving the New York Yankees, he is it. Al, who has exceptional talent, is responsible for the many outstanding publications concerning the team. He is the driving force behind the "Yankees" Magazine, and has done a number of Yankees books, projects, documentaries, etc. He unselfishly gave his time and valuable expertise to better this work, and I am very grateful to him. Al explained to me that use of the well-known "NY" symbol and the "Top Hat" logo of the Yankees, required the approval and permission of Major League Baseball.

Further arrangements were made, and I found myself in the New York headquarters of MLB where I met Don Hintze, Vice President of Publishing. I quickly learned Don was a special and kind person who relished the idea of "doing good things" for people who could use some hope and inspiration. Our fifteen-minute meeting turned into almost two hours as I related the origins of the project and highlighted what I envisioned to accomplish. We talked about our upbringings and the importance of providing the type of hope and inspiration that can make a difference. Don had come to the meeting prepared. He knew of the work of my Foundation, as well as the support of the Steinbrenner family and the New York Yankees for the book. More importantly, he knew MLB and the willingness of that outstanding organization to support worthy endeavors. With a handshake and a warm smile, he told me we had permission to go forward, and offered his personal availability to help in any way possible. Subsequently, he provided valuable input and guidance as we moved forward. Thank you so much Don and a huge thank you to Major League Baseball.

Before his passing, I was fortunate to talk with UCLA's wonderful and talented Coach John Wooden. He shared with me the principles he identified in his enlightening "Pyramid of Success." Authored in 1934, it remains an authoritative insight into personal accomplishment. I also sought input from others too numerous to mention who are recognized leaders and successes in various walks of life. I am grateful for the wisdom Coach Wooden provided, and to all those who helped out in that regard.

This project could not have succeeded without the core of the creative team that truly made the physical existence of the book a reality. Any undertaking of this magnitude requires a great effort and I was very fortunate to work with the creative team of Kelly Storm of Storm & Ford and Terry Zelen of Zelen Communications in the design and production aspects of this work. I was amazed and continuously appreciative of the depth of skills they consistently demonstrated over the long course of the meticulous and difficult efforts demanded. Just as impressive, Kelly and Terry showed incredible patience and perseverance in accommodating all of my many changes, revisions, and the difficult time schedules I imposed. Thank you both for your outstanding efforts to help me create and produce "The Making of a Championship Heart."

Of course, special thanks to Cindy Jameson, my trusted and invaluable personal assistant who has been with me for over two decades. She is always by my side and is an important part of my law practice, The Yerrid Foundation, and my recent ventures into the world of books. Invariably, Cindy does whatever is necessary and gives whatever it takes to promote success. I really cannot thank her enough for the tremendous amount of time she spent accomplishing the multiple tasks she undertook in helping me make this book and my vision a reality.

Lastly, I am eternally grateful and express my deepest personal thanks to the pediatric cancer patients, their families, caregivers, and the charitable organizations that have become so much a part of my life and made me a better person. It is my fervent hope this book will be of some benefit to these brave young warriors in their fight against this dreaded disease...

— STEVE YERRID

Photo by James LeClair

Framework Of The Book

This book was designed to capture key images from the Yankees' 2009 championship season, as well as selected photos from the past. Included are quotations from numerous Yankees players, ranging from Babe Ruth, Lou Gehrig, Joe DiMaggio, Mickey Mantle and Thurman Munson to Derek Jeter, Andy Pettitte, Jorge Posada, Alex Rodriguez and many more. The imagery and accompanying quotes relate to the particular quality being described. In most cases, the quotations came directly from the author's personal interviews with the players, coaches, and the Steinbrenner family.

Each chapter in the book highlights a specific trait or characteristic that is associated with becoming a champion – Preparation, Desire, Leadership, Attitude and Confidence, among others. A full palette of rich colors was used so that each trait has a defining background shade that creates easily identifiable chapters for the reader.

The photos follow the 2009 championship season from start to finish. For example, spring training pictures of the Yankees against the Phillies "lead-off" the book with Preparation being the first component featured. Fittingly, these same teams would eventually play each other at season's end in the World Series.

As the book progresses, images and quotations that focus on Challenge, Courage, Vision, Integrity, Pride and Respect are featured. The divisional and league championship games highlight other key qualities such as Hard Work & Determination and the importance of Perseverance.

The final sections focus on Teamwork, Tradition, Perfection and Heart as the Yankees become the World Series champions.

Scattered throughout the recent photographs are pictures of past greats shown in their glory days. The pictures of this older generation appear in sepia. The retired generation of Reggie Jackson, Wade Boggs, Tino Martinez, and Mike Mussina, to name a few, are reproduced in black & white.

A number of design features were added throughout, such as the home plate used to head each chapter, the famous Yankee Stadium frieze, and a "winning traits for life" emblem created for the opening page of the specific component highlighted. The traditional pinstripes of the Yankees appear on the inside covers. Photos of the new stadium and old stadium anchor the front and back of the book. This illustrates that while the Yankees have moved across the street and the "old" has been replaced with the "new", the winning tradition and beat of the championship heart goes on...

SunTide Publishing
Tampa, Florida

Created and Edited by Steve Yerrid
Additional Editing and Design by Kelly Storm, Storm & Ford,
Terry Zelen and James LeClair, Zelen Communications
Front and back cover photographs courtesy
of the New York Yankees

Library of Congress information on file with Publisher

ISBN 978-0-9832990-0-4

Printed in the USA
10 9 8 7 6 5 4 3 2 1

For more information on this book and to order additional copies,
go to www.championshipheart.com

THE MAKING OF A

CHAMPIONSHIP HEART

{ LESSONS LEARNED FROM BASEBALL & LIFE }

CREATED AND PRODUCED BY

STEVE YERRID

TABLE OF CONTENTS

TABLE OF CONTENTS

About George and the Book

The first time I met George Steinbrenner was over thirty years ago and remains vivid in my memory. It was what I like to call a "defining moment"... a time when a relationship or an event could go one way or another. As it turned out, that afternoon began a personal friendship that would last until his death.

John Germany, my mentor, and a senior partner in the prestigious law firm I had joined upon graduation from Georgetown, had sent me to a client meeting in his place. John was a founding partner in Holland & Knight, and one of the firm's established powers. He had an impressive list of clients that demanded and expected the very best of treatment. They ranged from Anthony Rossi, an Italian immigrant who began selling orange juice door-to-door and built that business into the multi-million dollar enterprise of Tropicana, to dynamic corporate leaders like George Steinbrenner, who took American Shipbuilding Company and parlayed it into the Yankees Empire.

We were seated at a large oval conference room table with probably twenty-five or thirty chairs surrounding it. Of course, George sat at the head and I learned quickly that when he was present, there was never any doubt as to who was in charge.

The discussion began as he took the issues point-by-point and sought input by going around the table from his left to right. After three or four of those assembled had given their views, I began to feel comfortable that by the time things got around to me, most of what needed to be said would already be covered, and I began to relax. That's when it happened.

One of the lawyers in the seated group of attorneys, advisors, and personal staff began to share his views and made the mistake by launching into a semi-lecture about what "had" to be done, and how George "needed" to act. I don't know to this day whether it was what he said or the way he said it, but George exploded. Catching the lawyer in mid-sentence, he stopped him cold. "I did not fly you down here to have you lecture me or tell me what I <u>have</u> to do. I'll decide that. I want advice. Advice, you understand!?!" (By now he was yelling.)

The room was hushed and the anger being expressed told me there was a history between the two that was not good. "And another thing, don't talk to me like I'm some kind of child that can't understand your legal jargon. If you can't help in a positive way, keep your mouth shut... I don't need a lawyer speech. I need to make a good decision and you are not helping."

A few more expletives followed and I decided to act. Looking back even now, it seems like I took an awfully big risk, but at the time I felt it was the right thing to do.

"Mr. Steinbrenner, may I talk with you for a moment?" The look on his face was a mixture of surprise and curiosity.

"Now?" he asked emphatically.

"Yes, sir," I said quickly. "It's important."

"It better be." His stern facial expression and stare said it before he did.

He got up and we walked out of the crowded conference room and into the hall. "What is it?" His tone gave nothing away.

I was a young trial lawyer, but I knew this was one of those gut check moments life sometimes deals out. "Mr. Steinbrenner, I realize who you are and understand we just met, but if you get around the table to me, I can't allow you to talk to me that way or we are going to have a problem." His face reddened and I braced myself for what was about to happen. What would I say to John? How could I explain blowing my first opportunity with one of the firm's most powerful clients?

He looked me over and said, "What are you? You some kind of hot shot?"

Before I could respond he slapped me on the back and his face broke into a big smile... "You are a hot shot. Hell, I like that. I respect that. Now, you're gonna be my hot shot. Let's go back in there and get some work done. Sit beside me and keep telling me what you think. I don't need another "yes" man. One more thing... call me George."

I'm not even sure I was breathing up until that point, but I remember exhaling as he turned to walk back in and I followed. Sure enough, I took the chair right beside him and as he continued going around the table, he paid me the greatest compliment I had received in my then early career by occasionally looking over after someone gave an opinion and asking "What do you think Hot Shot?"

I guess looking back it could have gone a lot differently, but it didn't. For the next three decades there was never a cross word, nor anything but the most genuine of friendships. We shared a mutual respect that I treasure to this day. Over the years, we had many experiences and conversations I will never forget. Often, as my career took off, George would be among the first to telephone congratulations over a courtroom victory or a newspaper story. He sometimes would send a short note that invariably started with the typed "Dear Steve" crossed through and a handwritten "Hot Shot" inserted as the salutation and sometimes signed by 'The Boss.' I have kept some of those special letters and they mean even more to me now that he's gone.

There are many stories I could tell of my friend... numerous acts of charity, kindness, and instances when he helped those in desperate need of a champion. Of course, I have heard the negativity surrounding George Steinbrenner. The criticisms, stories of his temper and his "bad side," etc... but I sure never saw it. 'The Boss,' as he became known to so many, helped more people and charitable causes than I could count – schools funded, hospital facilities built, financial assistance provided to the families of fallen law enforcement officers and the military, the huge sums raised over decades for the Boys and Girls Clubs of Tampa Bay... the list goes on and on.

I recall one instance particularly reflective of the George I knew. In 1992, after Hurricane Andrew struck the southern part of Florida and left a path of devastation and death in its wake, there was national media coverage of the critical and timely relief given by the Steinbrenner family and the New York Yankees organization. Not only were truckloads of supplies, food, clothing, and medicine sent – George took it upon himself to drive one of the loaded relief trucks to Miami (and back).

It was not a publicity stunt. In fact, he was upset the story even got out. With everyone aware of his rigid insistence on anonymity, I doubt anyone "leaked" his trucker's role. Most likely, it was simply one of the grateful recipients on the receiving end of the delivery that may have noticed a determined George Steinbrenner behind the wheel and unloading the much-needed supplies. Try as he might (even with his aviator sunglasses), I am certain George was not that hard to recognize. What the media never knew or reported was what happened when he got back to Tampa...

I had a long-scheduled fundraising event at my home and George had committed to come. After seeing him on the evening news and the television coverage about his trip, I was certain he would not be attending anything after driving all night. But I was wrong. Always on time (that usually meant 15 minutes early), George appeared at my door dressed in his familiar turtleneck and trademark blazer. "How you doin' Hot Shot?" he asked with a grin.

"I'm fine George, but what are you doing here? Your truck ride has been all over the news and I never figured you would show up after being up all night." It didn't come out the way I wanted, but he never broke stride.

"I told you I would be here and I am. I showered, shaved, and I'm ready to help out. Anybody here yet?" George said.

"No, you are the first", I managed to volunteer as I opened the door and he came in.

<figure>
New York Yankees

GEORGE M. STEINBRENNER III

YANKEE STADIUM
BRONX, NEW YORK 10451
TEL: (718) 293-4300

November 2, 2007

C. Steven Yerrid
The Yerrid Law Firm
101 East Kennedy Blvd.
Bank of America Plaza, Suite 3910
Tampa, Florida 33602-5148

Dear Steve: *Hot Shot*

In your short but storied life you have been:

- Recognized as one of the Top Ten Litigators in Florida
- Selected as Top Lawyer in the Nation
- Chosen as the Outstanding Lawyer of the Year in the Thirteenth Circuit
- Was named the Trial Lawyer of the Year, Tampa Chapter
- Made a member of the Inner Circle of Advocates
- An adjunct Professor at Stetson Law School
- A visiting Professor at Georgetown University Law Center

The list goes on and on and on. Today you add another feather to your cap with having been named the recipient of the prestigious *Perry Nichols Award*. Besides all this, you're just one "hell of a great guy".

Congratulations, and isn't winning fun!

Best regards,

George M. Steinbrenner III
Principal Owner
New York Yankees
</figure>

One of the many kind notes I received from George.

Well, not only was he the first to come, three hours later (after the final guest had departed), George was the last to leave. The event was a huge success.

Invariably, coupled with all the checks, the multitudes of gifted baseball tickets, and assorted charitable contributions to many different causes and people, was his insistence that he remain anonymous. That George was always there to give was impressive, but the way he did it made the goodness of his heart all the more special to me.

Frankly, I do not recall an occasion when I sought his help in some cause or another and he refused. And so it was with this project and The Making of a Championship Heart.

One day, we were talking about an upcoming event my Foundation was hosting to raise funds for pediatric cancer research. I shared my belief that people down and out probably needed hope and inspiration more than anything else. I "pitched" the idea of a book that used well-known sports figures people from all walks of life could relate to and embrace. I suggested the Yankees. Using an almost century of winning ways and a history of championships unequaled in professional sports, I expanded on the concept of using the players (both past and present) to convey the traits and characteristics it takes to be a champion on the field of athletics and, more importantly, in life.

Before I could go on, George interrupted. "I love the idea Hot Shot. I'm behind you and so are the Yankees. Now go do it, and do it right. Whatever you need, you got."

And so the journey began. True to his word, George and the Yankees opened every door for me. I had access to him, his family, and the team, as well as hundreds of photographs taken during their championship seasons. After his death, his sons Hal and Hank continued to support and encourage the project by giving me everything necessary to assure its successful completion.

The last time I saw George was at the Boys and Girls Clubs luncheon held in Tampa during March of 2010. The event is an outstanding and highly successful fundraiser that Hal Steinbrenner and the New York Yankees annually host during the final week of spring training.

After opening comments, introduction of the team, and a showing of the traditional Yankees highlight film, George was introduced. Sitting in his chair, he gave his familiar wave to the packed ballroom and the crowd exploded. He was acknowledged by cheers and a standing ovation that lasted several minutes and filled the air with an overwhelming loudness.

Just before lunch was served, I made my way over to George's table. I said a quick hello to his daughter, Jenny (who seemed to always be by his side), and talked with him briefly. He was very emotional about all that was going on around him. As I left we shook hands and he said, "Take care of yourself, Hot Shot..." Born on the 4th of July in 1930, he died eighty years later on July 13, 2010. The medical reports said his heart failed. While that may be factually accurate, the folks that cared for him would tell you that was not possible....

I think of him often and miss him greatly. To me, and many others, George Steinbrenner epitomized the heart of a champion and he made a positive difference in the lives of people. He still does.

Boss – this one is for you. Thanks for believing in me and this project. We did it.

– STEVE "HOT SHOT" YERRID

"I've seen the best of lawyers, and I put Steve right in that top list. He's a fighter, and odds don't bother him. I'd like him on my team any day. Early on, I said to myself if I was going to be in a fox hole I'd want him right next to me."

- GEORGE STEINBRENNER, 2003

PREPARATION

PREPARATION

prep·a·ra·tion

Noun

1: the action or process of making something ready for use or service or of getting ready for some occasion, test, or duty.

2: a state of being prepared; readiness.

WINNING
TRAITS
FOR LIFE

" Before anything else, preparation is the key to success.

— ALEXANDER GRAHAM BELL

A winning effort begins with preparation. "

— JOE GIBBS

"When I come to the stadium, yesterday is yesterday's news. I still prepare the same way, no matter what the outcome was. I don't take the bad game home with me. When I leave the stadium, I leave the results at the stadium."

– Jorge Posada

"I'm preparing from the off-season to that first game, and everything I do today will be in preparation for tomorrow. Everything that goes into my body, the exercise, the conditioning, the sleep I get tonight, that's all in preparation for tomorrow. And then tomorrow I will do it for the next day."

– Brian Bruney

"Yesterday's home runs don't win today's games"

– BABE RUTH

Joe DiMaggio

"If anyone wants to know why three kids in one family made it to the big leagues they just had to know how we helped each other and how much we practiced back then. We did it every minute we could."

— JOE DiMAGGIO

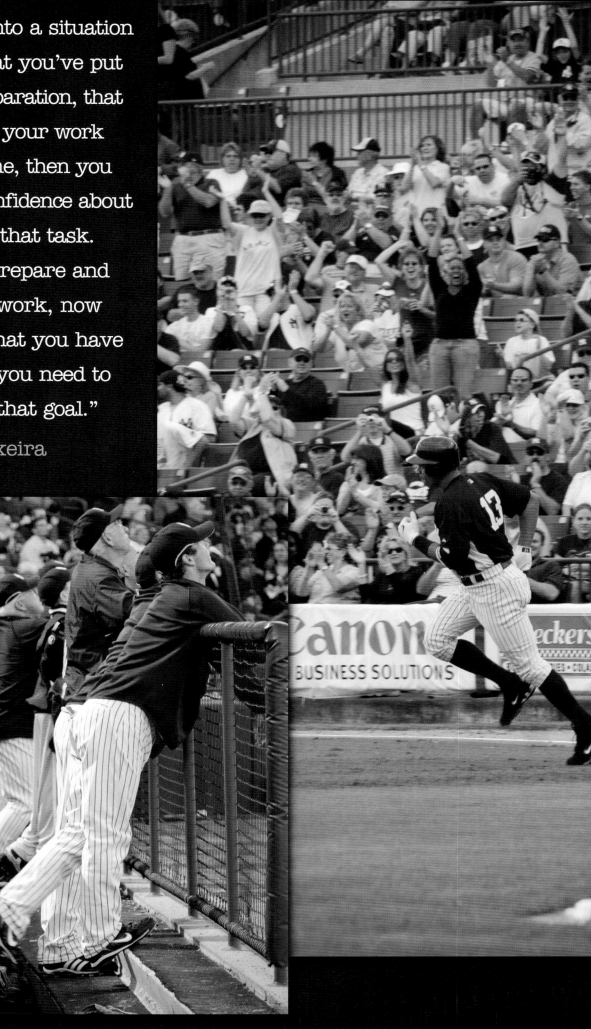

"If you go into a situation knowing that you've put in your preparation, that you've done your work ahead of time, then you get some confidence about performing that task. When you prepare and put in that work, now you know that you have everything you need to accomplish that goal."

– Mark Teixeira

"You hit home runs not by chance but by preparation."

– ROGER MARIS

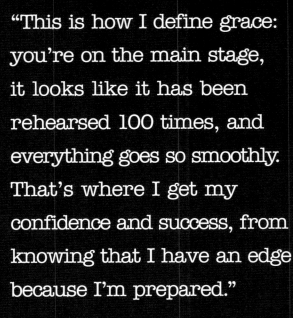

"This is how I define grace: you're on the main stage, it looks like it has been rehearsed 100 times, and everything goes so smoothly. That's where I get my confidence and success, from knowing that I have an edge because I'm prepared."

– Alex Rodriguez

DESIRE

de·sire

verb (used with object)
1: to wish or long for; crave; want.

TRAITS
WINNING FOR LIFE
THE MAKING OF A CHAMPIONSHIP HEART

> " Desire is the starting point of all achievement, not a hope, not a wish, but a keen pulsating desire which transcends everything.
>
> **— NAPOLEON HILL**

> Wheresoever you go, go with all your heart.
>
> **— CONFUCIUS**

> You can have anything you want if you want it badly enough. You can be anything you want to be, do anything you set out to accomplish, if you hold to that desire with singleness of purpose. "
>
> **— ABRAHAM LINCOLN**

DESIRE

"All I ever wanted to be when I was a kid was a ball player. I just always had that dream and determination that I wasn't going to let anything get in my way. Of course there are things that happen to you in life that you can't control, but the thing is to never lose sight of that dream and keep chasing it and don't let those obstacles get in the way."

– Jason Giambi

"How bad did I want to be a big leaguer? I always took on extra work, and was the last one to leave practice. I probably worked harder than most, to the point that some people thought I was crazy. I think the guys that didn't make it, that had more talent than me, those are the guys who I just out-worked."

– Jorge Posada

"Everyone loves a winner. Winners are a select group and to be one you should want to be one. Don't ever be afraid to try to get to the next level."

— RON GUIDRY

"It was all ▶ I lived for, to play baseball."

— MICKEY MANTLE

"A loser only goes through the motions. Dedication and desire to win makes you a champion."

– RICHARD MONTELEONE

"Winning ▶ isn't everything. Wanting to win is."

– Jim "Catfish" Hunter

"I believe in my case it was the desire I had to be the best player I could be that made the difference. I wasn't always the fastest runner, didn't have the best arm but I was always a good hitter and I worked really hard day in and day out, year in and year out, to try and be the best I could possibly be. I knew through the hard work and great effort of everyday working out and practicing that nobody could stop me from achieving my goal."

– Tino Martinez

CHAMPIONSHIP HEART

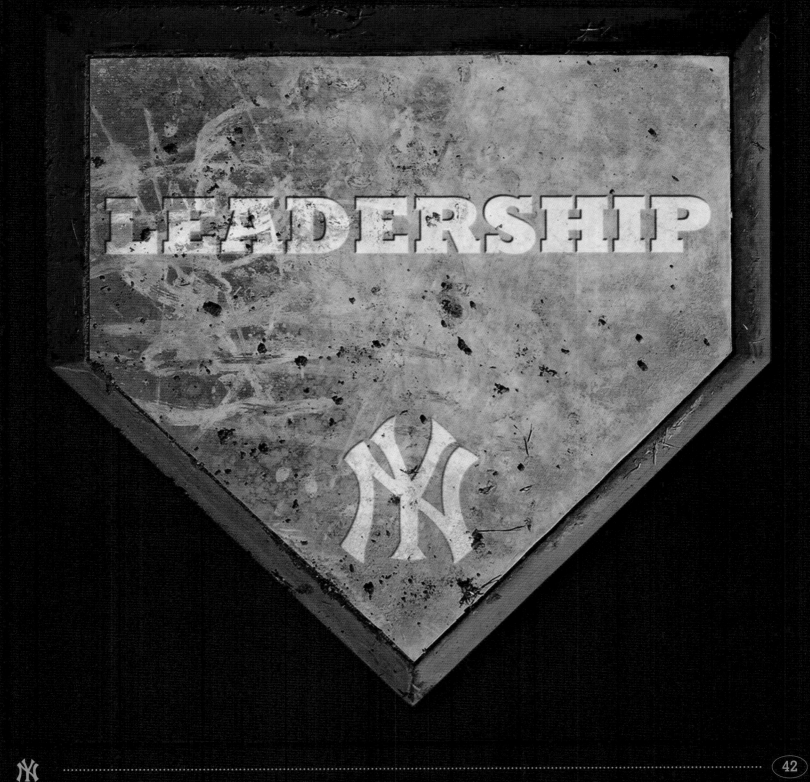

LEADERSHIP

LEADERSHIP

lead • er • ship

Noun

1: the position or function of a leader.

2: ability to lead.

3: an act or instance of leading; guidance; direction.

> *If your actions inspire others to dream more, learn more, do more and become more, you are a leader.*
>
> **– John Quincy Adams**

> *Do not go where the path may lead. Go instead where there is no path and leave a trail.*
>
> **– George Bernard Shaw**

> *Leadership is based on a spiritual quality; the power to inspire others to follow.*
>
> **– Vince Lombardi**

"You would always see him on the field, talking to the players, telling them he wanted to win. Most of the team owners, you never see them down there, but he would come down and talk and it was a great inspiration. Not only on the field, but off the field, with the Boys and Girls Clubs. He was the guy that everybody knew as a winner and a great person."

– Robinson Cano

"What Dad did, when he made money to pack the houses across the country with a great team, was put the money back into it. Because what his core was, what he wanted this team to know was, I believe in you and I'm going to give you the best team on the field."

– Jenny Steinbrenner Swindall

"The rate of the pack is determined by the speed of the leader."

— GEORGE STEINBRENNER

"The greatest manager has a knack for making ballplayers think they are better than they think they are."

– REGGIE JACKSON

"Leadership has to have integrity. If a leader doesn't have integrity people aren't going to believe in him. You can't put yourself in a room and say I'm the leader and I'm above it. You have to work hard to give the people in that room with you a better life. Not just their life on the field, but off the field as well."

– Joe Girardi

"A person always doing his or her best becomes a natural leader, just by example."

— JOE DIMAGGIO

"Leadership is
a role you have
to earn in order
to be effective."

– ALEX RODRIGUEZ

"There are two types of leaders. One leads by being vocal and outspoken, and the other leads by example."

— WADE BOGGS

"I like hitting fourth and I like the good batting average. But what I do every day behind the plate is a lot more important because it touches so many more people and so many more aspects of the game."

— Thurmon Munson

"I liked the way Munson played the game. He was a leader first, a teammate second, and whatever he did on the field was second to him. He wanted everyone to feel comfortable. He wanted everybody to be on the same page, ready for every game."

— Jorge Posada

"If you can't sit in the saddle,
you can't lead the charge."

— GEORGE STEINBRENNER

THE MAKING OF A
CHAMPIONSHIP HEART

ATTITUDE

ATTITUDE

at·ti·tude

Noun

1: manner, disposition, feeling, position, etc., with regard to a person or thing; tendency or orientation, esp. of the mind.

TRAITS WINNING FOR LIFE THE MAKING OF A CHAMPIONSHIP HEART

"

Ability is what you're capable of doing.
Motivation determines what you do.
Attitude determines how well you do it.

– LOU HOLTZ

Our attitude toward life determines
life's attitude towards us.

– EARL NIGHTINGALE

Believe and act as if
it were impossible to fail.

– CHARLES KETTERING

"

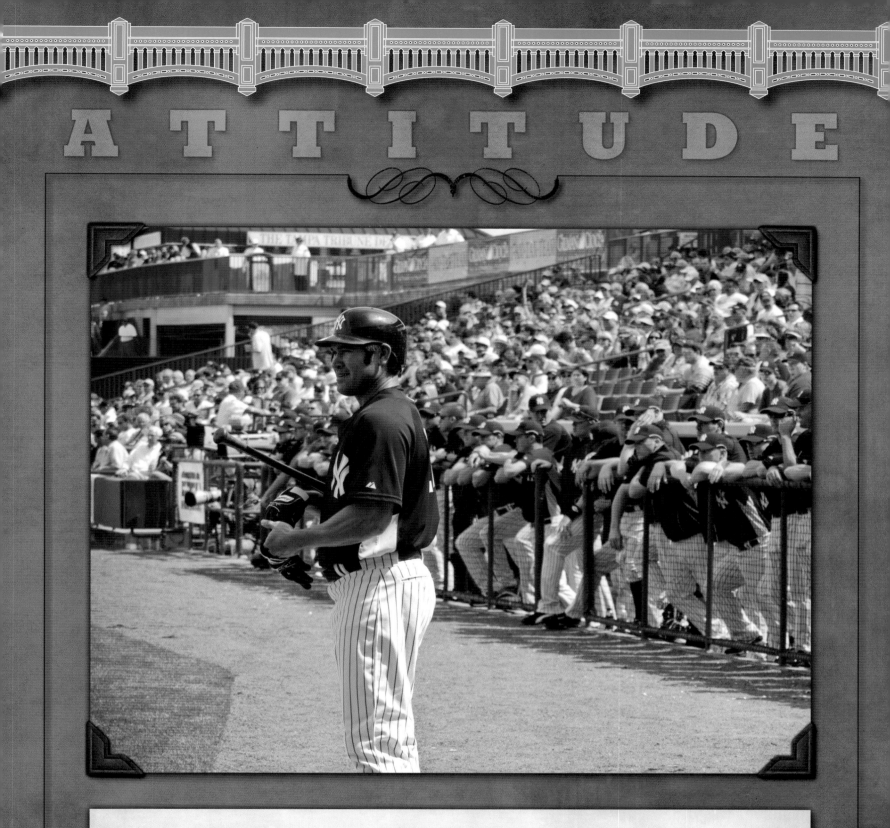

"In the game, there are a lot of things you can be upset about, but making an out in baseball doesn't compare with what some people have to deal with. I try to look at life and enjoy every minute of it. I've been playing baseball since I was six and to be able to still play – I couldn't ask for anything better. That's why every day I have to smile about what I'm doing."

– Johnny Damon

"One time I said 90% of the game is half mental! What I meant was everything, or mostly everything, is all in your head. Your attitude and your mental skills are more important than anything. If you have the right attitude, whether playing ball or working hard, there's no limit to what you can do."

– Yogi Berra

"We can't just go there and play around. We have to go there with the mentality that we have to win."

– Mariano Rivera

"Good things don't just happen, you have to make them happen – attitude is everything."

– "Goose" Gossage

"Stay positive. A positive outlook has a tremendous effect on a person's physical well-being."

— HANK STEINBRENNER

"Our lives are not determined by what happens to us but how we react to what happens, not by what life brings us, but the attitude we bring to life."

"A positive attitude causes a chain reaction of positive thoughts, events and outcomes. It is a catalyst and it sparks extraordinary results."

– Wade Boggs

"You gotta have fun. ▶
Regardless of how
you look at it,
we're playing a game.
It's a business,
it's our job, but I
don't think you can
do well unless you're
having fun."

— **DEREK JETER**

"Never give up. You can never give up on your dreams and your goals — on life at all, you just can't give up. If you keep working hard and have a positive attitude throughout any situation you are going through, you will have a better chance of getting through it."

— Tino Martinez

"Attitude plays a big role... huge. I keep my alarm clock in the side dresser drawer next to my bed because every day I want to wake up with a smile on my face. I don't need an alarm clock – I want to get up because I'm going to get to do something that I love every single day."

– Nick Swisher

"The first day I was here last year, I'm getting ready and I'm nervous, and I look up and see a sign that says 'Winning isn't everything, it's second… to breathing'. I like having that will to win. There's something about wearing a Yankee uniform that gives you a never-say-die attitude."

— Nick Swisher

"I'll take any way to get into the Hall of Fame. If they want a batboy, I'll go in as a batboy."

— PHIL RIZZUTO

"I consider myself the luckiest man on the face of the earth. And I might have been given a bad break, but I've got an awful lot to live for."

– Lou Gehrig

THE MAKING OF A

CHAMPIONSHIP HEART

DETERMINATION

de·ter·mi·na·tion

Noun

1: the act of coming to a decision or of fixing or settling a purpose.

2: the quality of being resolute; firmness of purpose.

3: fixed direction or tendency toward some object or end.

> A dream doesn't become reality through magic; it takes sweat, determination and hard work.
>
> **— COLIN POWELL**

> The difference between the impossible and the possible lies in a person's determination.
>
> **— TOMMY LASORDA**

> The price of success is hard work, dedication to the job at hand, and the determination that whether we win or lose, we have applied the best of ourselves to the task at hand.
>
> **— VINCE LOMBARDI**

HARD WORK &
DETERMINATION

"I try to live my life with this little slogan — that no one will ever take my job because they work harder. One thing that we can't control is the gift we have from up above, but we can control what we do with those gifts and how hard we work."

— Joe Girardi

"Nothing is given to you. Work hard at everything you do. The harder you work, the more you are going to benefit. There are no shortcuts."

— DEREK JETER

"Enjoy your sweat because hard work doesn't guarantee success, but without it, you don't have a chance."

– ALEX RODRIGUEZ

"My father always told me that when you do something give it your all. Work hard at it because if you do have a talent in there or you do want to become successful or complete a task, you have to work hard to get there. It's not always going to be easy, there's a lot of sacrifice, there's a lot of long days, but in the end when you accomplish your goal or when your team accomplishes its goal that hard work all pays off."

— Mark Teixeira

"I'm always working hard, trying to get better every year. I don't want to do the same thing every year. I want to keep getting better and better."
– Robinson Cano

"Live every day as if it's a gift, because nobody
is promised tomorrow. Live every day as hard as you can,
be determined, set your goals and never give up."

— YOGI BERRA

"Hard work and determination are essential in doing anything that matters. As an organization and as a baseball team, I never want to be outworked or have anyone want to succeed more than us."

– GEORGE STEINBRENNER

"Never quit regardless of anything that you're doing – don't back down, don't be scared to take a chance on something, and if things aren't going well, work your tail off to get better. I think the major factor for me getting here has been my work ethic. I may not be the most talented guy, but it's going to be pretty doggone hard to outwork me. Whatever it is you're going to do, work to be the best at it."

– Nick Swisher

"Determination is just something you have to have in life. Whether you're a school teacher or a baseball player – every-body in life – you have to have determination to be a better teacher, to be a better player, to be a better individual."

– CC Sabathia

"There's a difference between just your average player or even your average good player, your normal good player, and the great clutch players or the great clutch people in any line of work, any walk of life. To become a champion, to succeed at something, you have to have that attitude of determination and never quit and willpower, and accept the need to trust in people."

– Hank Steinbrenner

"Since I was a young kid, I was bound and determined to play baseball. I loved the game from the first time I saw it and loved it every time I ever played it, no matter the outcome. Every time Dad would come home from work I would have the bat, ball and glove to play. He knew it was important to me and so it was important to him."

– Don Larsen

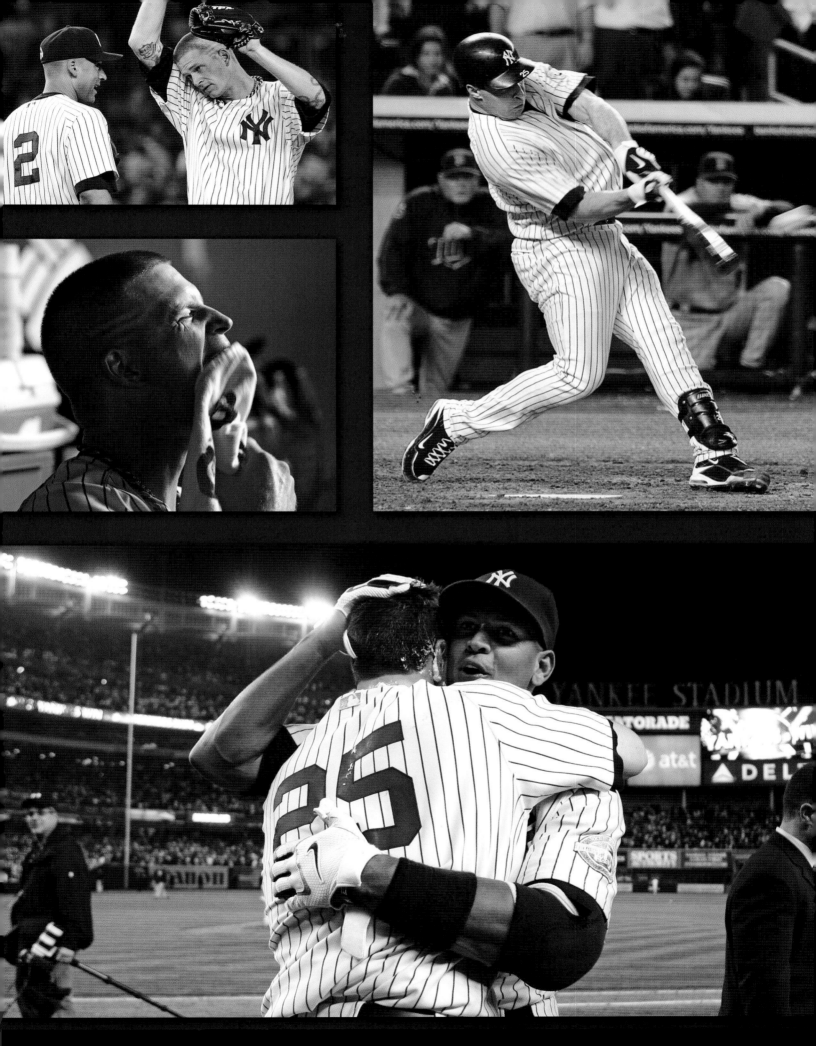

"You don't just accidentally show up
at the World Series."

– DEREK JETER

CONFIDENCE

CONFIDENCE

con • fi • dence

Noun

1: full trust; belief in the powers, trustworthiness, or reliability of a person or a thing.

2: belief in oneself and one's powers or abilities; self-confidence; self-reliance; assurance.

3: certitude; assurance.

"We gain strength, and courage, and confidence by each experience in which we really stop to look fear in the face... we must do that which we think we cannot.

— ELEANOR ROOSEVELT

Besides pride, loyalty, discipline, heart, and mind, confidence is the key to all locks."

— JOE PATERNO

"Believing is a big part of achievement. If you believe you can achieve something then you will."

– Alex Rodriguez

"I always have confidence... It's big. It's good to win."

— MARIANO RIVERA

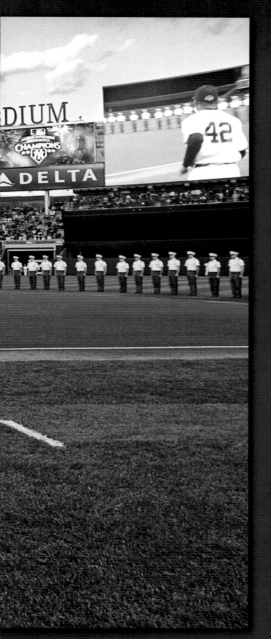

"Watch my dust."

— BABE RUTH

"I like the ball in a big game. I'm not afraid to take it."

— David Wells

"It's important when you're growing up to have someone around to encourage you, whether it's a teammate or family. I signed the contract to play baseball before I left high school so I played with more mature guys and always got advice from them, from the moment I played my first game through my major league career. I loved it and worked hard at it. I had some bad days, but even the best have bad days. I just never gave up because my team-mates had confidence in me and I had confidence in them."

– Don Larsen

"Somewhere along the line somebody told me I could do this and I actually believed them. I learned that if some- body gives you motivation and you actually believe what they are telling you than you can push yourself hard enough and have enough desire to achieve more than you thought you could before."

– Mike Mussina

"To be a champion you must have a drive to get it done and the belief and confidence in yourself to know that you are going to get it done and get out of a tough situation. Believing in yourself and having the determination to know that you prepared hard and worked up to this day, and when you get into tough situations you know to draw from that."

– CC Sabathia

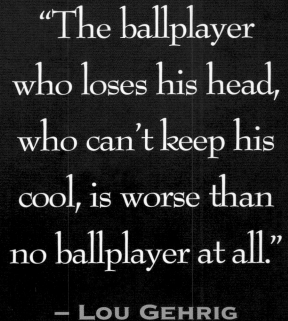

"Talent is not all of it.
It's more how you carry yourself,
how you play the game hard."

— DEREK JETER

"The ballplayer
who loses his head,
who can't keep his
cool, is worse than
no ballplayer at all."

— LOU GEHRIG

"Always follow your dreams, don't let anyone tell you that you can't be something."

— ALEX RODRIGUEZ

"Success is as simple as when we think good things, good things happen."

– "Goose" Gossage

"You've got to have confidence...
remember the good ones. Watch the
good ones. It's all about positive
thinking, taking everything and looking at it with the right point of view.

– A.J. Burnett

THE MAKING OF A
CHAMPIONSHIP HEART

EFFORT

EFFORT

ef • fort

Noun
1: exertion of physical or mental power.
2: an earnest or strenuous attempt.
3: something done by exertion or hard work.

> "Be willing to give that extra effort
> that separates the winner from the one
> in second place.

– H. Jackson Brown Jr.

> Effort only fully releases its reward
> after a person refuses to quit.

– Napoleon Hill

> There is no comparison between
> that which is lost by not succeeding and
> that which is lost by not trying."

– Francis Bacon

"I had a father who played in the big leagues for 10 years. He never forced me to play baseball; he didn't care what I was, all he wanted me to do was give 150% to being the best I could be at whatever it was. And you know what, baseball was my calling, and he told me, 'Hey, you gonna play some ball!'"

– Nick Swisher

"To compete at the highest level it takes an awful lot of effort, not only physical effort but mental effort and concentration and focus."

— ANDY PETTITTE

"Effort is everything. Vince Lombardi, probably the greatest coach in the history of sports, period, said winning isn't everything but the effort to win is. It's crucial to life and in sports. We don't hang onto our players very long at the Yankees if they don't give 100% effort."

– Hank Steinbrenner

"Somebody once asked me if I ever went up to the plate trying to hit a home run. I said, 'Sure, every time.'"

— MICKEY MANTLE

"As a competitor, you always want to do your absolute best; you want to have no regrets. You always want to be able to say, 'I gave it everything I had, and if I didn't win, I'll try harder the next time'."

— Yogi Berra

"I've always thought that if I give it my all, in the end if it doesn't work out it wasn't meant to be. I can live with putting in the work and giving it 100% and it not working out. I know I've done everything I could do."

— Mark Teixeira

"I think you have to be able to accept for every winner there is a loser, and you have to go out there with your all. At least you can lay your all on the line and whatever the outcome is, you can look at yourself in the mirror that night or after the season and say, 'I gave it everything, I've played like a champion, everything I put into this I left out on the field'."

– Johnny Damon

"I'm just a ballplayer with one ambition, and that is to give all I've got to help my ball club win. I've never played any other way."

— JOE DIMAGGIO

"I played the game one way. I gave it everything I had. It doesn't take any ability to hustle."

– WADE BOGGS

"Don't accept being the fourth or fifth outfielder. Don't accept being the long relief. Push each other. Take someone's job."

— JOE GIRARDI

"I haven't always done a good job, and I haven't always been successful — but I know that I have tried."

— George Steinbrenner

"If my uniform doesn't get dirty, I haven't done anything in the ball game."

— Rickey Henderson

"Losing is part of the game and sometimes losing makes you better. As long as you tried your best and played your best you can't ask any more of yourself."

– Ron Guidry

"I swing big, with everything I've got. I hit big or I miss big. I like to live as big as I can."

— BABE RUTH

CHAMPIONSHIP HEART

CHALLENGE

CHALLENGE

chal·lenge

Noun

1: a call or summons to engage in any contest, as of skill, strength, etc.

2: something that by its nature or character serves as a call to battle, contest, special effort, etc.

> " Most of the important things in the world have been accomplished by people who have kept on trying when there seemed to be no hope at all.
>
> — **DALE CARNEGIE**

> The most glorious moments in your life are not the so-called days of success, but rather those days when out of dejection and despair you feel rise in you a challenge to life, and the promise of future accomplishments.
>
> — **GUSTAVE FLAUBERT**

> The ultimate measure of a man is not where he stands in moments of comfort and convenience, but where he stands at times of challenge and controversy. "
>
> — **MARTIN LUTHER KING, JR.**

"You have to look at things as a challenge, the same way as you look at a baseball game. In athletics, and in life, regardless of who you are, how successful you are and what you do — you are going to be faced with challenges. I think that you have to stare those challenges in the eye and try to make the most of them."

– Derek Jeter

"I have definitely been through some serious heartache in my life, and some serious trials where I felt like I would not be able to make it through. But you learn from them, and I feel like I've been a better man when I have come out the other side. Through it all, faith has been my constant companion and I am never alone."

– Andy Pettitte

"In life, you know those kinds of hands that you get dealt – all 2's if you will; come back and turn it into aces."

– REGGIE JACKSON

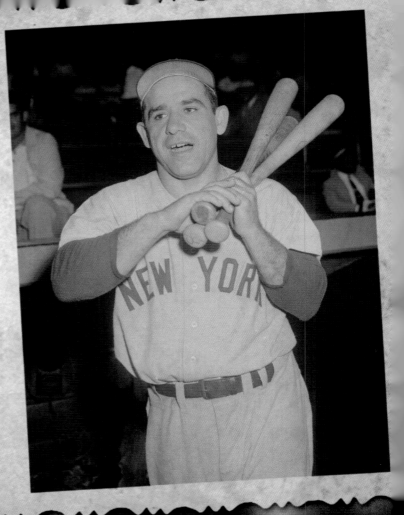

"Baseball is a democratic game. Anyone can play, doesn't matter how big or strong you are, you just have to work at it. There are also great lessons in baseball — how you respond or bounce back from disappointment. It teaches you a lot about yourself."

– Yogi Berra

"Sometimes you have to
slip and fall to realize how to
pick yourself up again."

– JESSICA STEINBRENNER

"When you think everything is going wrong and everything is turning the wrong way, it's happening for a reason. Going through tough times makes you a better person — a stronger person."

— Jorge Posada

"There were several times that I wanted to quit when I was going through adversity. I had never experienced it in high school and then I got to the big leagues and had some trouble. I just really had to sit down and ask myself, do I want this? Do I want to be a professional baseball player? Do I want to live this life? And if I do I need to suck it up and try to get through it. I think me growing up playing baseball as a kid, its something I always wanted to do. It really made me realize that when I struggled."

— CC Sabathia

"Every strike brings me closer to the next home run."

— BABE RUTH

"In baseball as well as in life there are tough times. In baseball, when you play well and your hitting is good, it's all good. But when you're doing bad, and you're in the slump and making outs, and things aren't going so well, you really just have to have that fire and drive to keep it going – the work ethic to not give in to failure and be the best that you can be."

– Tino Martinez

> "Life is about obstacles, endeavors in life are not to be overlooked."
>
> — WADE BOGGS

"Each mistake should be a lesson. Try not to make that same mistake again and improve the failed experience. Ultimately the goal is for all of us to work together because we are trying to get to that finish line."

— Felix Lopez

"Everyone has a breaking point, turning point, stress point… the game is permeated with it. The fans don't see it because we make it look so efficient. But internally, for a guy to be successful, you have to be like a clock spring, wound but not loose at the same time."

— Dave Winfield

"I expect our players to do what we all must do in every aspect of life. Meet challenges head on, reach deep inside, and make the moment an opportunity to succeed."

— George Steinbrenner

THE MAKING OF A
CHAMPIONSHIP HEART

COURAGE

COURAGE

cour • age

Noun

1: the quality of mind or spirit that enables a person to face difficulty, danger, pain, etc., without fear; bravery.

TRAITS

> The bravest are surely those who have the clearest vision of what is before them, glory and danger alike, and yet notwithstanding, go out and meet it.
>
> **— THUCYDIDES**

> The greatest test of courage on earth is to bear defeat without losing heart.
>
> **— ROBERT GREEN INGERSOLL**

> All our dreams come true – if we have the courage to pursue them.
>
> **— WALT DISNEY**

"You've got to have courage. We talk about teamwork, we talk about being strong, and never giving up, but you have to have courage, you have to have inspiration, and you have to have that desire to move on day in and day out."
– Mariano Rivera

"No one knows the inner strength of a human being. Hope and family and the will to live can carry people through."

– Joe Girardi

"You're a special person when you make it through the toughest times. You become a giant in character, a giant in God's world and a giant in life. You become a giant on the real team of life and that's God's team."

— Reggie Jackson

"Courage is not giving up. Everyone hits a hurdle, everyone loses or fails sometimes. What you learn, what you create out of it — that's what matters."
– Yogi Berra

"You can't be afraid to fail. You are going to fail in anything that you do, but any mistakes you make you try to learn from them and you try not to make that same mistake twice... I think even in terms of adversity you can learn things and you can turn a negative into a positive."

– Derek Jeter

"Courage is what makes you not afraid to fail. Even if things aren't bright one day, you can turn it around because you know in your heart you can do better."

– Ron Guidry

"A team is where
a boy can prove
his courage on his own.
A gang is where a
coward goes to hide."

— MICKEY MANTLE

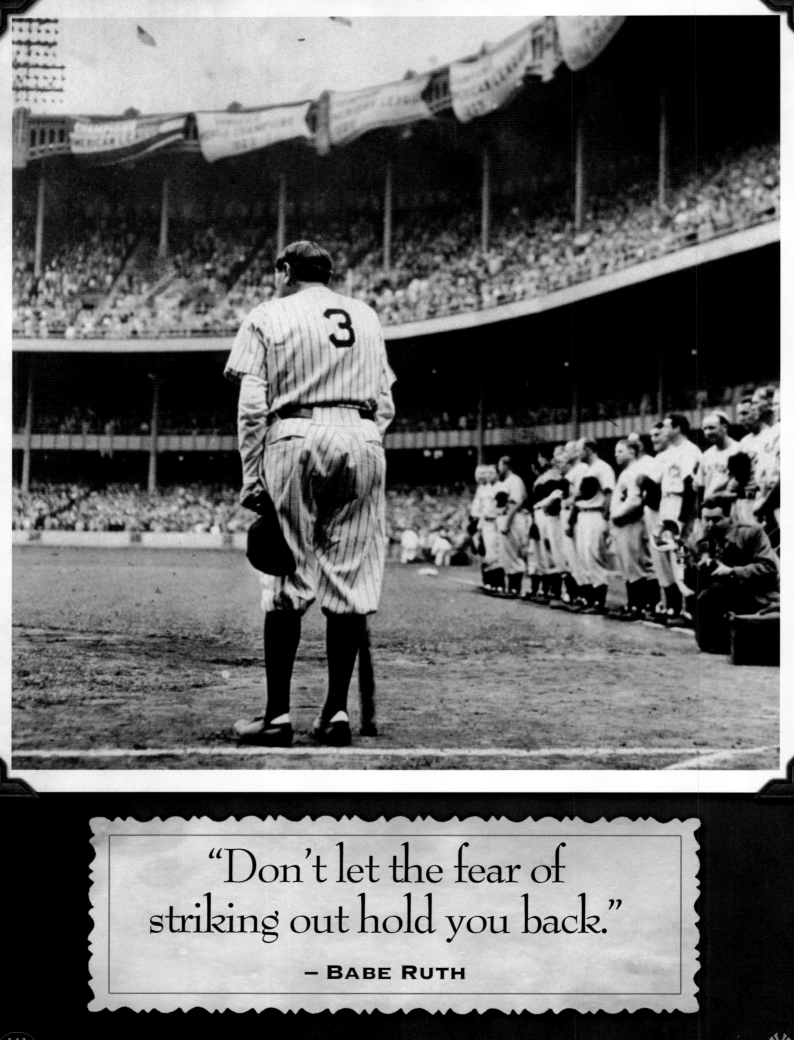

"Don't let the fear of striking out hold you back."

– BABE RUTH

PERSEVERANCE

PERSEVERANCE

per·se·ver·ance

Noun

1: steady persistence in a course of action, a purpose, a state, etc., esp. in spite of difficulties, obstacles, or discouragement.

TRAITS
WINNING FOR LIFE

"*Our greatest glory is not in never failing, but in rising up every time we fail.*

— **Ralph Waldo Emerson**

Fall seven times, stand up eight.

— **Japanese Proverb**

Our greatest weakness lies in giving up. The most certain way to succeed is always to try just one more time."

— **Thomas Edison**

PERSEVERANCE

"This team as much as any that we've ever had, there's never been a team that showed more persistence, in never giving up. Never giving up if they've got injuries, never giving up if guys are in slumps, never giving up if they're ten runs down in the game. This team just doesn't give up, they fight, fight, fight."

– Hal Steinbrenner

"You can never give up. I always say, God never gives you something that you can't carry. Everybody is going to go through a tough situation; it's going to make you a better person or a better athlete or a better man. If you don't go through those situations you won't know what you are capable of doing. Even the greatest in the world go through a slump... that's why you have to work harder and just say to yourself, 'I can do this'."

– Robinson Cano

"There's no doubt that there's times when you feel like you need to give up, but for me personally, my faith is the main thing I call upon. I feel like God created me and I have a special purpose for my life, and that requires me not giving up and not quitting at all."

– Andy Pettitte

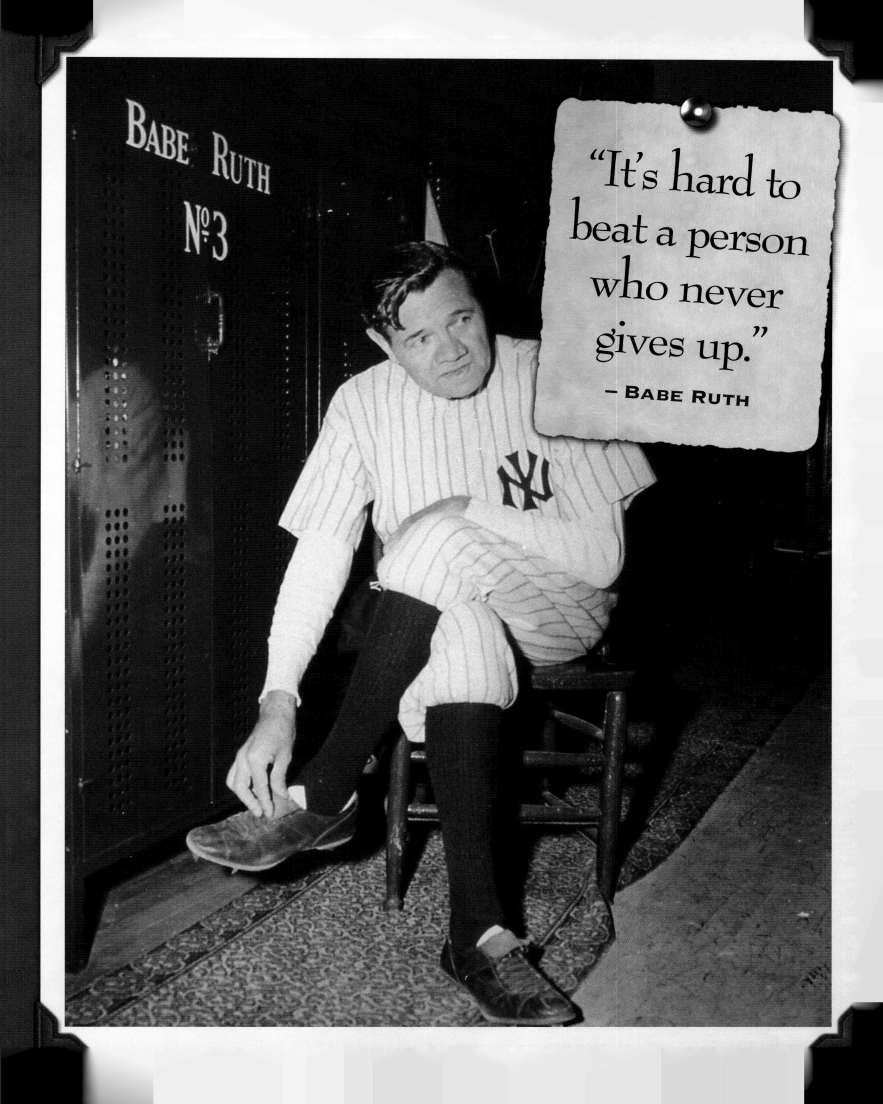

"Never give in to whatever you're up against. I've always said that every lesson of life is experienced on the baseball field. Perseverance takes dealing with failure, but we can learn from our failures. When you fall on your face you pick yourself back up again."

– "Goose" Gossage

"I was raised to believe 'no quitting'. Quitting was just not allowed by my father. If I started a sport, then I was going to continue with that sport as long as I could make the team. He constantly drove into us to never quit."

– Jessica Steinbrenner

"It's never over. You don't want to be in the position to be down four runs in the ninth inning, but it's not over until the last out."

— DEREK JETER

"I think for us baseball is a little like life. There's always going to be good days and there's always going to be challenging days. The guys in this game that can keep their head, keep motivated and keep moving forward when things aren't going well, those are the guys who succeed."

— Mike Mussina

"Never give up... when things are hard, when things are tough, never give up on those opportunities. When you are always persistent and always give your best and fight for everything, you will succeed."

– Mariano Rivera

"Quit really isn't in my vocabulary. I don't think I have ever got anything from quitting."

— MARK TEIXEIRA ▶

"Never, ever give up.
As I said, nothing's
over 'til it's over.
Every person's life
has a purpose."

– YOGI BERRA

CHAMPIONSHIP HEART

VISION

VISION

vi • sion

Noun

1: the act or power of sensing with the eyes; sight.

2: the act or power of anticipating that which will or may come to be.

WINNING TRAITS FOR LIFE

THE MAKING OF A CHAMPIONSHIP HEART

> Just because a man lacks the use of his eyes doesn't mean he lacks vision.
>
> **– STEVIE WONDER**

> The best vision is insight.
>
> **– MALCOM FORBES**

> It is a terrible thing to see and have no vision.
>
> **– HELEN KELLER**

"Have a light at the end of the tunnel. Understand that when you get through to the other side you're going to be a stronger person. Then set your goal and keep working on it. You have to have a vision in life and not let anyone take that away from you."

– Joe Girardi

"You can see a lot just by observing."

— Yogi Berra

your mind of what you want – that's half the battle – then visualize what you want. Then go after it and never give up. Make a choice that you are not going to stop until you achieve your goal and never take your eye off the ball."

– Alex Rodriguez

"There's no question about it.
Think small, concentrate on doing the small
things and the big things will come."

— ALEX RODRIGUEZ

"Take care of the things you can control. As long as you have a bat in your hand, you can rewrite the story."

— REGGIE JACKSON

"Good hitters just don't go up and swing. They have a plan. Call it an educated deduction. You visualize. You're like a good negotiator. You know what you have, you know what he has, and you try to work it out."

— Dave Winfield

"Everyone's been given a gift. We don't always know exactly what that gift is when we're young, but as we get older we realize that there are certain things we're drawn to. I think once you figure out what you enjoy, what your job is, or whether its school or whatever it may be, that it's very important to work hard at it and get the most out of your ability – out of your gift."

– Mark Teixeira

Things in life have to start with a dream. In order to be successful in life, you don't have to dream big, but just have a dream."

— WADE BOGGS

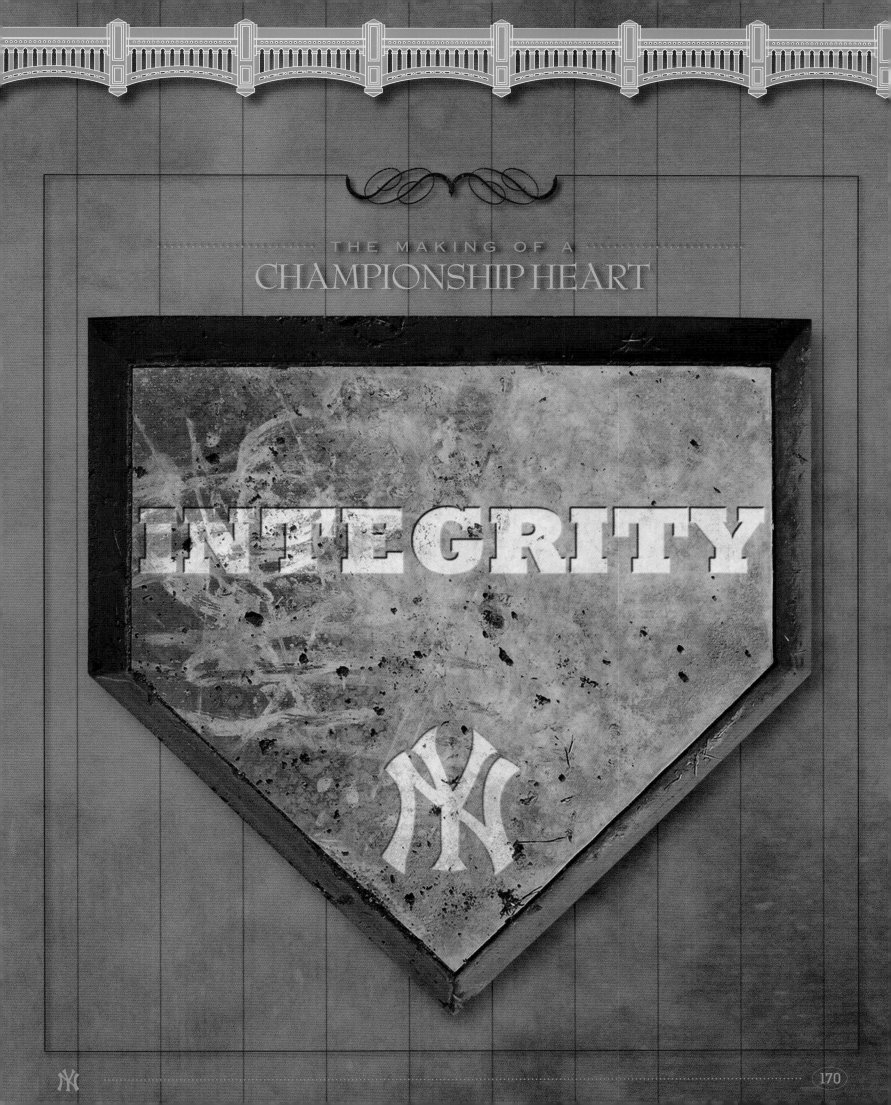

THE MAKING OF A
CHAMPIONSHIP HEART

INTEGRITY

INTEGRITY

in·teg·ri·ty

Noun

1: adherence to moral and ethical principles; soundness of moral character; honesty.

2: the state of being whole, entire, or undiminished.

THE MAKING OF A CHAMPIONSHIP HEART
WINNING TRAITS FOR LIFE

" Real integrity is doing the right thing, knowing that nobody's going to know whether you did it or not.

— Oprah Winfrey

Be more concerned with your character than your reputation, because your character is what you really are, while your reputation is merely what others think you are.

— John Wooden

The time is always right to do what is right. "

— Martin Luther King, Jr.

"It is very easy to be in your own world and do things for yourself. But in the end, when your life is over and it's all said and done, its going to be the relationships you've had and how you've touched other people that are the most important things. Helping others and just being a good example and a helping, loving person is very important."

– Mark Teixeira

"The most important thing to me — and my father and mother passed that along to me — is honor and integrity. If you cannot look at yourself in the mirror and know that you're doing the right thing then how do you live your life and how do you pass that on to others?"

– Jenny Steinbrenner Swindall

"I have always drawn my strength from my family and faith. Never gave up in anything, never will."

— YOGI BERRA

"A lot of times we consider things important that are not important. But when you have that inner feeling that family and things you leave behind are much more important than material things, it makes you keep going and work harder to be able to leave your mark in life."

— Felix Lopez

"Just strive every day to be the best that they can be. Be the best player and be the best person you can be."

— CC SABATHIA

"My parents were always there for me, in good times and tough times, and spent hours and hours helping me practice. Out on the field I'd make three errors, and then look over and they're in the stands, pulling for me. They always took time for the needs of me and my sister."

– Jorge Posada

"Family is always number one to me, it has been since I was born and it still is now. I was brought up the right way and hopefully one of these days I'll have my own son or daughter and I'm going to teach him or her all the things that I've learned."

— Nick Swisher

"If my father told you what meant more to him than anything in the world, it's his family, and he showed us that nothing else in the world means more than that. He did by example and he told us, share your moments with your kids."

— Jenny Steinbrenner Swindall

"You have to find something that makes you happy and find something you feel is important. After winning a world championship, what I found was important was sharing my story and telling them the ride I had, which ever since I was a kid, wasn't always smooth. But you have to just keep going through life and enjoying every stage that you have because it is something very precious. There is always something out there that is worse than what you are going through."

– Johnny Damon

THE MAKING OF A

CHAMPIONSHIP HEART

GIVING BACK

GIVE

give

Verb

1: to present voluntarily and without expecting compensation; bestow.

2: to place in someone's care.

WINNING TRAITS FOR LIFE

> You give but little when you give of your possessions. It is when you give of yourself that you truly give.

— KAHLIL GIBRAN

> From what we get, we make a living; what we give, however, makes a life.

— ARTHUR ASHE

> It's not how much we give but how much love we put into giving.

— MOTHER TERESA

"You give of a pure heart. If you have to do something so that you get credit for it, it's wrong because it's not of pure heart. You do things for people because you have a good heart and it isn't for any other reason."

– Jenny Steinbrenner Swindall

"There were a couple of things I got from my parents – first of all, love. But they also worked extremely hard to give us a better life. My parents worked three jobs and my mother worked all of them while she was dying from cancer, but the thing was that they were always there for us and they always wanted a better life for us. I think as a community we should always want a better life for the generation to follow."

– Joe Girardi

"We have a responsibility not just as athletes, but as members of society, to treat people well. To do things the right way."

— ALEX RODRIGUEZ

"We have a lot of blessings in our lives. And it's our duty to give back as much as we can to the community in a variety of different ways. My dad did so much that nobody knows about, that only his close friends know, and a lot of those things involved the Boys and Girls Clubs. He called children this country's greatest natural resource – and he was right."

– Hal Steinbrenner

"I grew up in the Boys & Girls Club, grew up in the inner city, saw everything that it can do for you. I was fortunate to be able to get out, and now I'm trying to give back."

– CC Sabathia

SEC   ROW   SE
39
SUITE LEVEL

"Try to
live every day
to the fullest and
make a difference
in people's lives."

— YOGI BERRA

"The ability to have is so you can do things for others. If you can do things for others who are less fortunate, then it will come back to you."

— GEORGE STEINBRENNER

THE MAKING OF A

CHAMPIONSHIP HEART

PRIDE &
RESPECT

PRIDE

pride

Noun

1: a high opinion of one's own dignity, importance, merit, or superiority, whether as cherished in the mind or as displayed in bearing, conduct, etc.

2: the state or feeling of being proud.

3: self-respect; self-esteem.

> If you believe in yourself and have dedication and pride, and never quit, you'll be a winner. The price of victory is high but so are the rewards.
>
> **— PAUL BRYANT**

> Generosity is giving more than you can, and pride is taking less than you need.
>
> **— KAHLIL GIBRAN**

> Every human being, of whatever origin, of whatever station, deserves respect. We must each respect others even as we respect ourselves.
>
> **— U. THANT**

"Respect, looking appropriately, acting appropriately... that was absolutely huge to my father. He often said to our players, 'You are a Yankee — you are wearing the pinstripes, you need to have pride in what you do.'"

— Jessica Steinbrenner

"I come out here every day, and my job is important when it comes to being there every day and being there for my pitchers. Every time I go out on the field, I take a lot of pride in what I do at the plate, but I take a lot more pride in what I do behind the plate."

– Jorge Posada

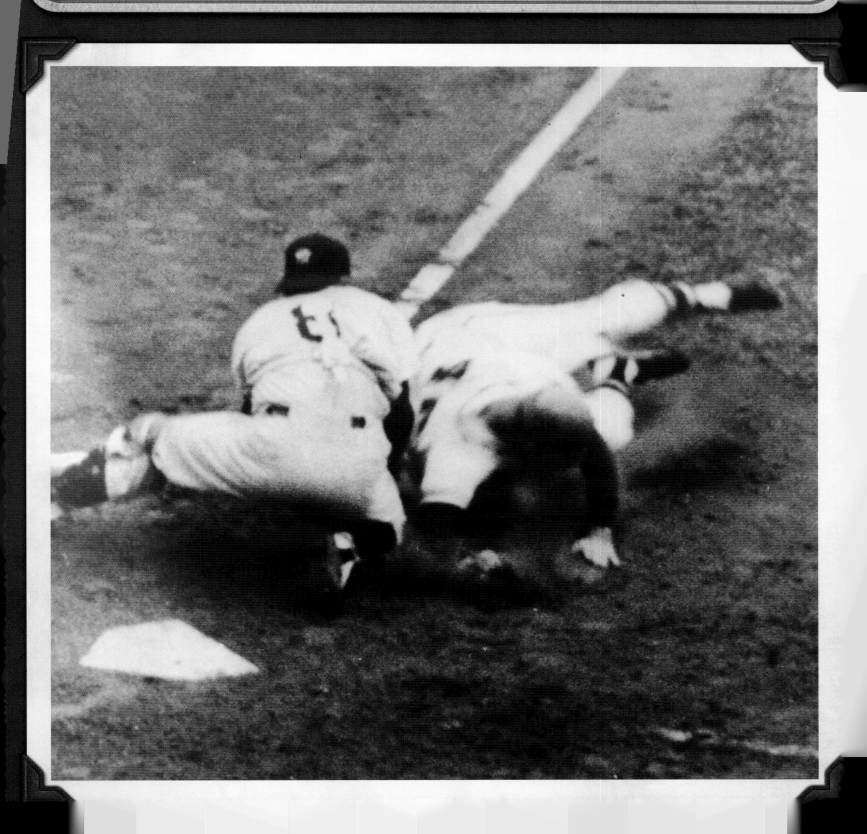

"I like to have my hand on every single plate that goes out. It's really a good feeling when someone compliments your meal, and you had everything to do with making it. It's very rewarding."

— Bill Dickey

"There is always some kid who
may be seeing me for the first or last time,
I owe him my best."

— JOE DIMAGGIO

"Be respectful. Treat people the way you want to be treated. Respect the lowest rank and the highest rank and you'll never get in trouble."

— ALEX RODRIGUEZ

"A championship ▶
is only a trophy,
being as good
as you can be and
proud of what you
have accomplished is
the best reward."

– RON GUIDRY

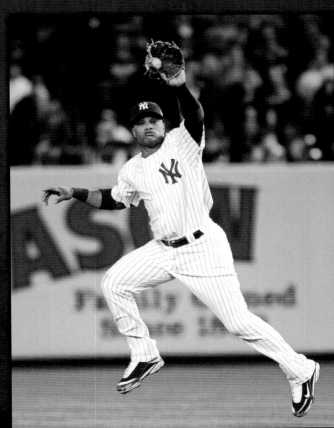

"It's important that we treat the game with respect and push ourselves to not stop playing just because it doesn't look good. You never know what's going to happen — you may get a lucky call, a bad bounce that goes your way… eight guys in a row may get base hits. It's a strange game and strange things happen and you never know, so you just never quit. Because once in a while you pull one of those games out."

— Mike Mussina

"God, I hope I wear this jersey forever."

— DEREK JETER

TEAMWORK

team • work

Noun

1: cooperative or coordinated effort on the part of a group of persons acting together as a team or in the interests of a common cause.

2: work done with a team.

> Individually, we are one drop.
> Together, we are an ocean.
>
> — RYUNOSUKE SATORO

> Individual commitment to a group effort – that is what makes a team work.
>
> — VINCE LOMBARDI

> Alone we can do so little; together we can do so much.
>
> — HELEN KELLER

"Teamwork is everything. Vince Lombardi said it best when he was coaching; everything is about fundamentals, execution, determination and teamwork. It's important.'"

– Hank Steinbrenner

"It's a team effort. I've had a lot of bad days in ball but you just don't want to give up, I don't care how bad it is. There's going to be some good days and if you work hard enough and believe in yourself and your team-mates, you're going to have some good things happen to you."

— Don Larsen

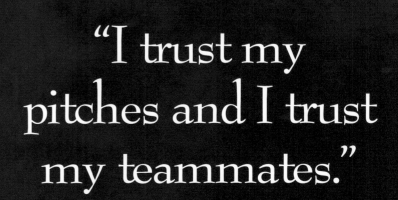

"I trust my pitches and I trust my teammates."

— MARIANO RIVERA

"I always felt on championship teams, it wasn't about the individuals. I always felt that if I was a good team player and supported my teammates when they were going through tough times, and by the same token do my job and keep everybody positive through the down time, then we could be a more successful team. I felt that's what our team had through the championship years. It didn't matter who the hero was as long as we were all together in this thing — fighting for one goal, then achieving that goal."

– Tino Martinez

"Teamwork is very, very important. You can accomplish more with others than by yourself."

— ALEX RODRIGUEZ

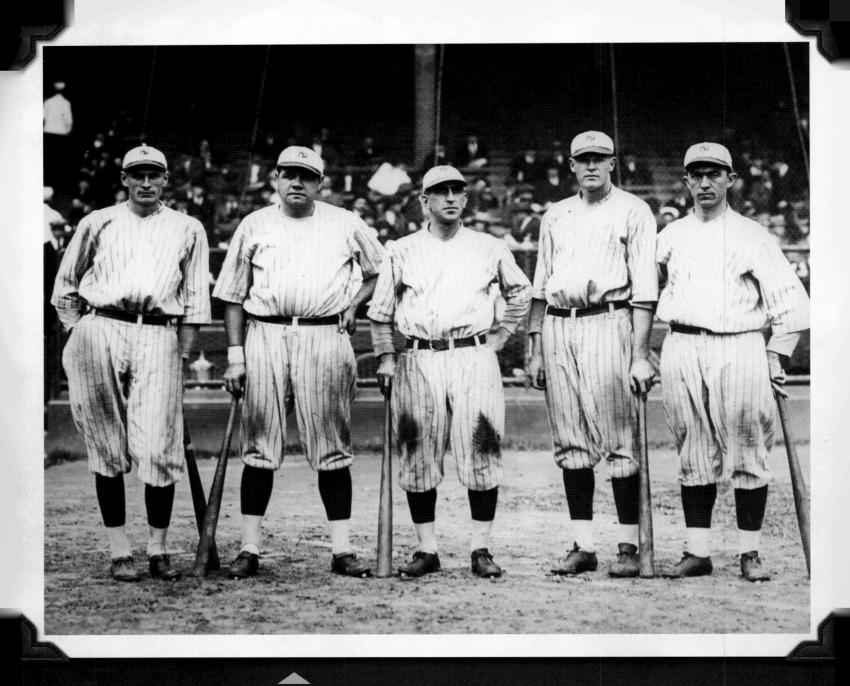

"The way a team plays as a whole determines its success. You may have the greatest bunch of individual stars in the world, but if they don't play together, the club won't be worth a dime."

— BABE RUTH

"Teamwork… it's about chucking your ego at the door and doing what's best for the good of the team. It's the ability to work together even when times are tough, because people show their true colors when times are tough. It's easy to be a winner when things are good, but teamwork and support from your team-mates helps you be a winner when things are tough."

– Joe Girardi

"Being in the clubhouse with all of the guys that have won so much, it gives you confidence that all you have to do is go out and do your part, and you have a good chance to win."

– CC Sabathia

"How I fit in, I don't know, I just know what I did could help others. That's what I always tried to do – make my team better."

– Yogi Berra

"I felt like I was a piece of a big puzzle – I had to do my job but I was only a piece of it. We drew strength from everyone around us."

– "Goose" Gossage

"You have to be willing to sacrifice yourself for the good of the team."

— RON GUIDRY

"It doesn't mean that much unless the team wins. Individual goals are great, but if I'm watching the playoffs, it won't mean much."

— MARK TEIXEIRA

"It's important how a team deals with adversity. I misjudged a fly ball last night and dropped it, and the first thing the guys said to me when I came in the locker room was, 'Hey man, it's alright, we'll get it later.' The thing about being on this team that is so amazing is you have all these huge names in this locker room and everybody pulls for each other. Everybody has each others' back and I think that's a major factor here and that you have to have in all aspects of life."

– Nick Swisher

"I think on a championship team everybody is in the same boat. Everybody is pulling at the same time, pulling for one goal, and supporting each other. As a team leader, when you see something wrong or you see a bad apple, obviously you have got to make these people realize that everyone must pull in the same way and for each other. If someone is not doing that, you've got to surround him and pull him back into the team, so that bad apple turns into a good apple. "

– Jorge Posada

"When you're talking about a team, it's not always what role you're best suited for, it's what's going to help the club. Clubs need flexibility."

— JOE GIRARDI

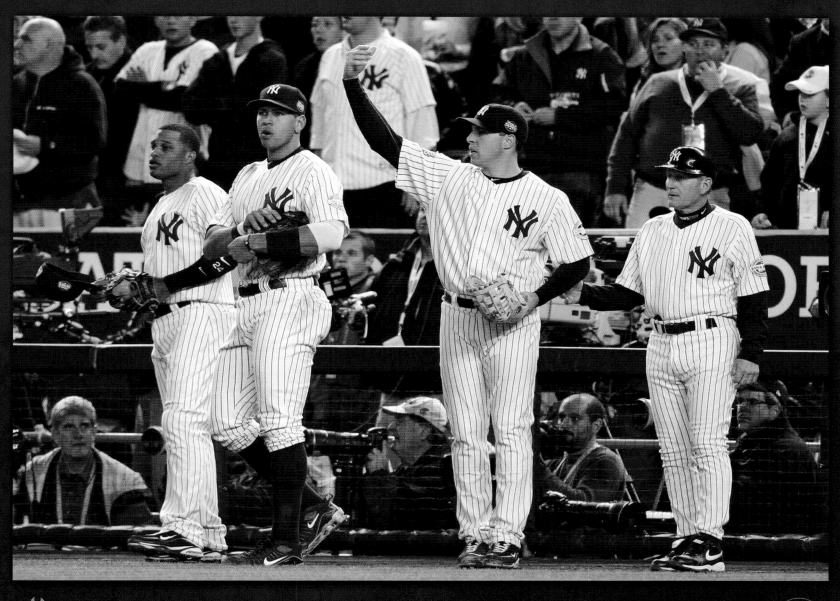

"Teamwork is every-
thing. With teamwork,
you don't just count on
yourself — you can count
on each other and feel
good in being account-
able to every one of
your teammates."

– Mariano Rivera

"I have always been a very passionate player and person. I often wear my emotions on my sleeve, sometimes for better, sometimes for worse. I hope that my teammates always respect that of me, as I trust they know my commitment to winning."

– A.J. Burnett

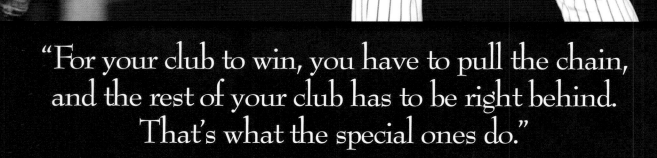

"For your club to win, you have to pull the chain,
and the rest of your club has to be right behind.
That's what the special ones do."

– REGGIE JACKSON

TRADITION

TRADITION

tra·di·tion

Noun

1: the handing down of statements, beliefs, legends, customs, information, etc., from generation to generation.

2: a long-established or inherited way of thinking or acting.

> " It takes an endless amount of history to make even a little tradition. "
>
> — HENRY JAMES

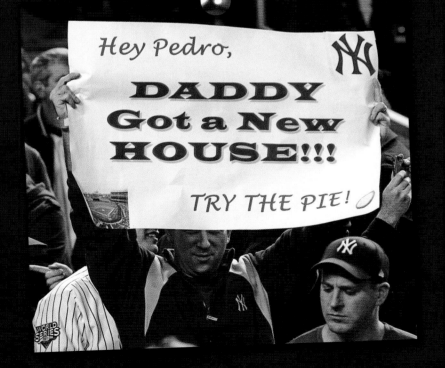

"Yankee Stadium. Things go on here. You can write a book about it."

— ANDY PETTITTE

"When I came to the Yankees, that's when I became a champion... because everyone here wants the win."

— ROBINSON CANO

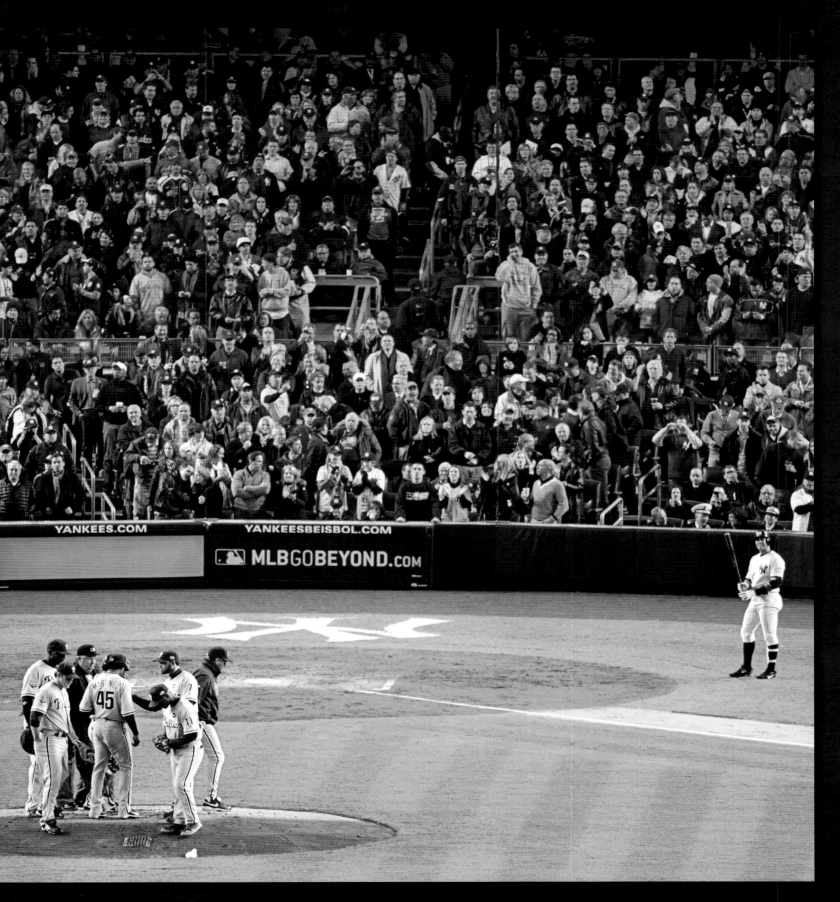

"To be a Yankee is a thought in everyone's head... Just walking into Yankee Stadium, chills run through you. I believe there was a higher offer, but no matter how much money is offered, if you want to be a Yankee, you don't think about it."

— Jim "Catfish" Hunter

"Everybody feels real fortunate just to have a big league uniform on, but there really is something about putting on the pinstripes that just automatically gives you a little shot of pride."

– Paul O'Neill

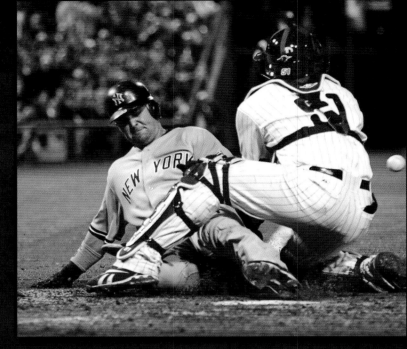

"I have the greatest
job in the world. Only
one person can have
it. You have shortstops
on other teams – I'm
not knocking other
teams – but there's
only one shortstop on
the Yankees."

– Derek Jeter

"You kind of took it for granted around the Yankees that there was always going to be baseball in October."

– WHITEY FORD

"I'm like a fan. I live with the Yankees and I die with the Yankees."

— GEORGE STEINBRENNER

"Every day I come to the ballpark, I thank God that I'm wearing this uniform, for giving me the opportunity to be successful and last that long. To pitch that long, and do it good, for the New York Yankees... it's great."

– Mariano Rivera

"I'd like to thank the good Lord for making me a Yankee."

— JOE DIMAGGIO

"With our rich history, our fans transcend the generations. You walk around Yankee Stadium sometimes during the game and you'll see children, and you'll see people in their seventies and eighties that have been coming to the games since the 1940's. Our fans appreciate that we have them foremost in mind, that if we do spend money on a free agent, or on our player development system to get these great kids and to build these great kids, we're doing it for them. They expect a winner and we expect that of ourselves."

– Hal Steinbrenner

"When you're entrusted with a tradition, you've got to protect it."

– GEORGE STEINBRENNER

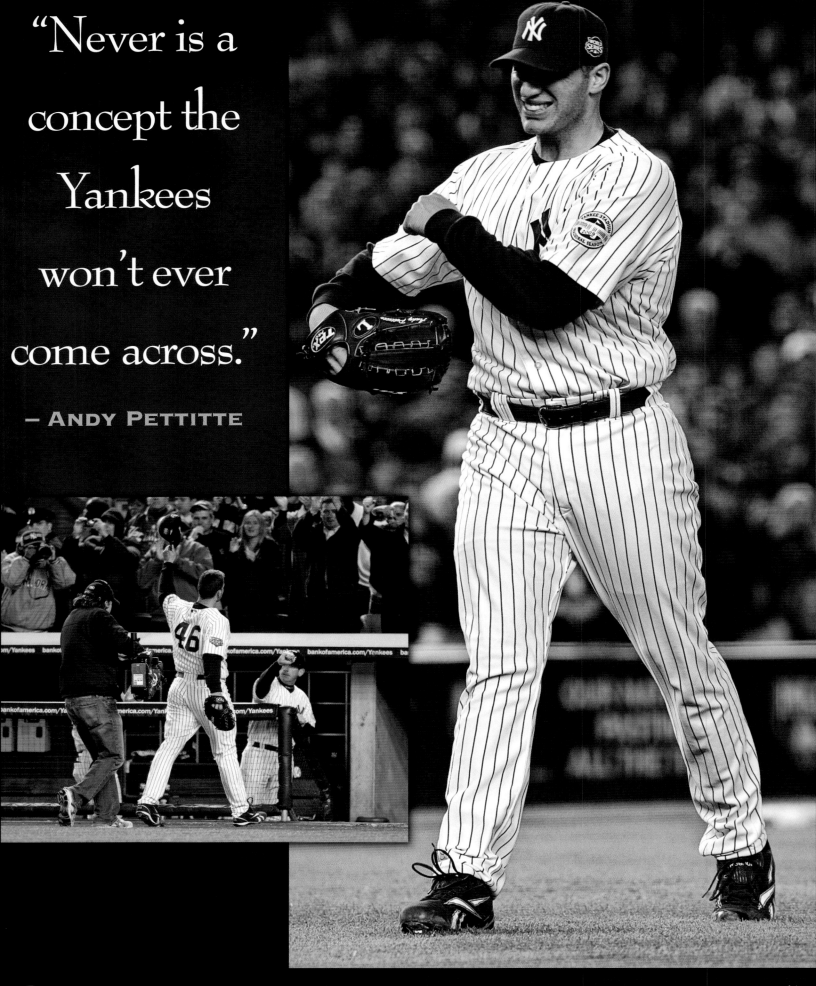

"Never is a concept the Yankees won't ever come across."

— ANDY PETTITTE

"My heroes,
my dreams, and my
future lie in Yankee
Stadium and they can't
take that from me."

— DEREK JETER

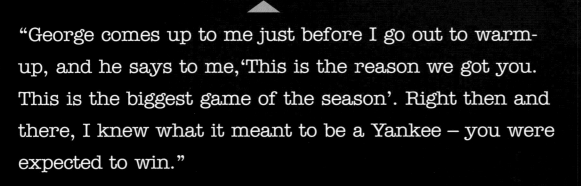

"George comes up to me just before I go out to warm-up, and he says to me, 'This is the reason we got you. This is the biggest game of the season'. Right then and there, I knew what it meant to be a Yankee – you were expected to win."

– Tommy John

"They may call me 'The Boss', but in the end, to succeed as owner of the Yankees, you have to be a servant – a servant to the history and legacy of the Yankees."

– George Steinbrenner

"When I was a little boy,
I wanted to be a baseball player
and join a circus.
With the Yankees
I've accomplished both."

— GRAIG NETTLES

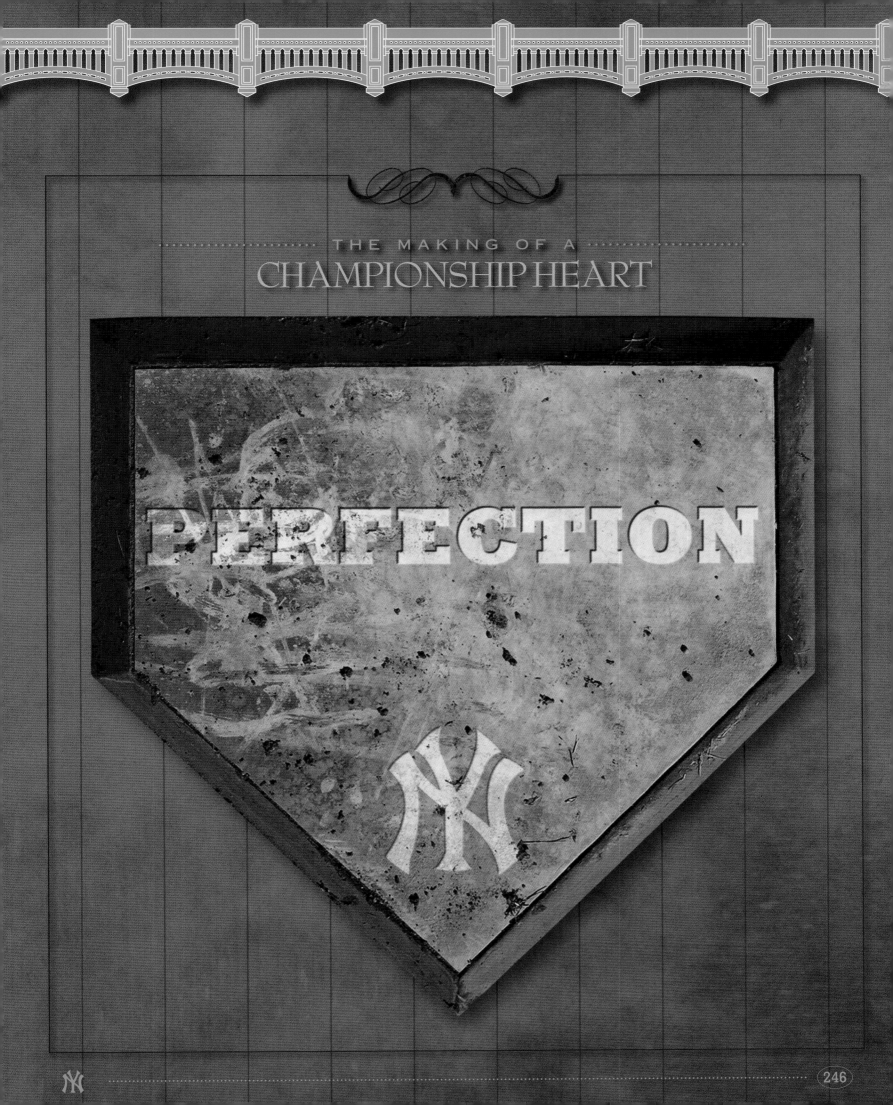

THE MAKING OF A
CHAMPIONSHIP HEART

PERFECTION

PERFECTION

per·fec·tion

Noun
1: the highest degree of proficiency.
2: the highest or most nearly perfect degree of a quality or trait.
3: the act or fact of perfecting.

TRAITS
WINNING FOR LIFE

> " Perfection is not attainable, but if we chase perfection we can catch excellence.
>
> **— VINCE LOMBARDI**

> Perfection consists not in doing extraordinary things, but in doing ordinary things extraordinarily well.
>
> **— ANGELIQUE ARNAULD**

> I am careful not to confuse excellence with perfection. Excellence, I can reach for; perfection is God's business. "
>
> **— MICHAEL J. FOX**

"Winning is the most important thing in my life, after breathing. Breathing first, winning second."

– GEORGE STEINBRENNER

"Once you play at this level, winning is important. Anybody can go out there and lose, but to me learning how to play is learning how to win."
— Joe Girardi

"I like to think of the world's greatest athlete coming up to bat against me — Tiger Woods, Wayne Gretzky, I don't care who it is — and I'm looking at him thinking, you have no chance."
— David Cone

"Everybody is entitled to a good day. No matter if it's in sports, marriage, your first born, or if somebody's good at it — two good days! I was very fortunate being with the Yankees and to have that day I did in the World Series. I pitched a perfect game. How could it get any better than that?"
— Don Larsen

"Winning the World Series Championship is like a dream — you can't get any higher than that in sports. But you can always do greater things in life."
— Yogi Berra

"To pitch a perfect game wearing pinstripes at Yankee Stadium, it's unbelievable. Growing up a Yankee fan, to come out here and make history, it really is a dream come true."
— David Wells

"There's not one guy that's going to stand up every single night... we want to get it from everyone. That's how we are going to win."
— Jorge Posada

"In the beginning I used to make one terrible play a game. Then I got so I'd make one a week and finally I'd pull a bad one about once a month. Now, I'm trying to keep it down to one a season."

— Lou Gehrig

"You do whatever
you have to do to win.
Everything that's ethical
and moral that
you can do, that's what
you do, period."

— HANK STEINBRENNER

"You play the game to win the game, and not to worry about what's on the back of the baseball card at the end of the year."

– Paul O'Neill

> "If you're going to play at all, you're out to win."

— DEREK JETER

	1	2	3	4	5	6	7	8	9	10	R
PHILLIES	0	0	1	0	0	2	0	0	0		
YANKEES	0	2	2	0	3	0	0	0			

GATORADE

"I don't mind
getting beaten, but I
hate to lose."

— REGGIE JACKSON

"Whatever I do, I love to win. I don't care if its tennis or ping pong, I'll kill myself to win it."

—ANDY PETTITTE

"Winning it once makes you want to win more. To be able to get a chance to do it again, that's all you can ask for."

— CC Sabathia

HEART

heart

Noun

1: anatomy. a hollow pump-like organ of blood circulation, composed mainly of rhythmically contractile smooth muscle located in the chest between the lungs and slightly to the left and consisting of four chambers.

2: the center of the total personality, esp. with reference to intuition, feeling, or emotion.

3: the vital or essential part: core.

> Great hearts steadily send forth the secret forces that incessantly draw great events.
>
> **– RALPH WALDO EMERSON**

> The best and most beautiful things in the world cannot be seen or even touched. They must be felt with the heart.
>
> **– HELEN KELLER**

> Nothing is impossible to a valiant heart.
>
> **– JEANNE D'ALBRET**

"You can give an athlete everything they need to prepare but it still may come down to that one moment where they're inspired greatly by something... it's that single moment of greatness where two great athletes or athletic teams are competing and one just has that moment of greatness that puts him beyond the other one."

– Jessica Steinbrenner

"My proudest part of winning five consecutive championships was just being part of something special. To me, all of us had a champion's heart, otherwise we wouldn't be champions. We truly pulled for each other, every minute, every day, all the time."

– Yogi Berra

"The difference between a championship heart and that of just another competitor is a willingness of giving yourself up for the team. Willing to give that effort and give whatever yard of understanding it takes to win. As a catcher you can really go 'O' for four or 'O' for five and still win a ball game and still feel pretty good about yourself. You've gone in the game and helped out this pitching staff to accomplish what you want... a win for the team!"

– Jorge Posada

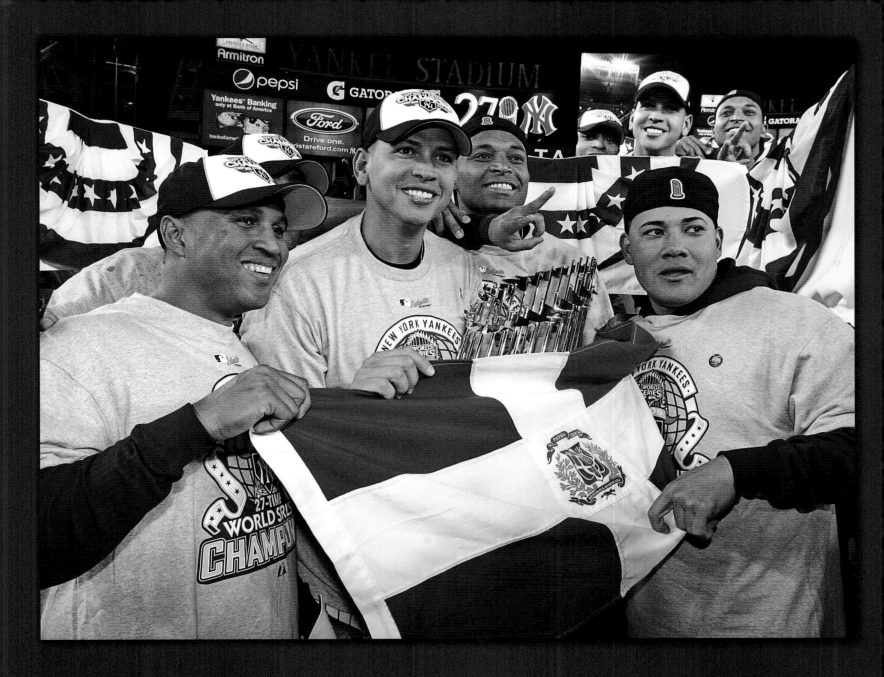

"What makes a champion? The difference is hard work, dedication, passion for whatever you are doing, whatever you are trying to battle...whatever you are trying to defeat. Being not necessarily worried about results, just worried about the climb and the battle and how you go about your work, and your passion."

– ALEX RODRIGUEZ

"The difference between what we do and what other people who want to do what we do is that we just have a little more in us — there's something in us that keeps us pushing at it a little bit harder and striving to be better than we ever thought we could be — to be more than we ever thought we could be."

– Mike Mussina

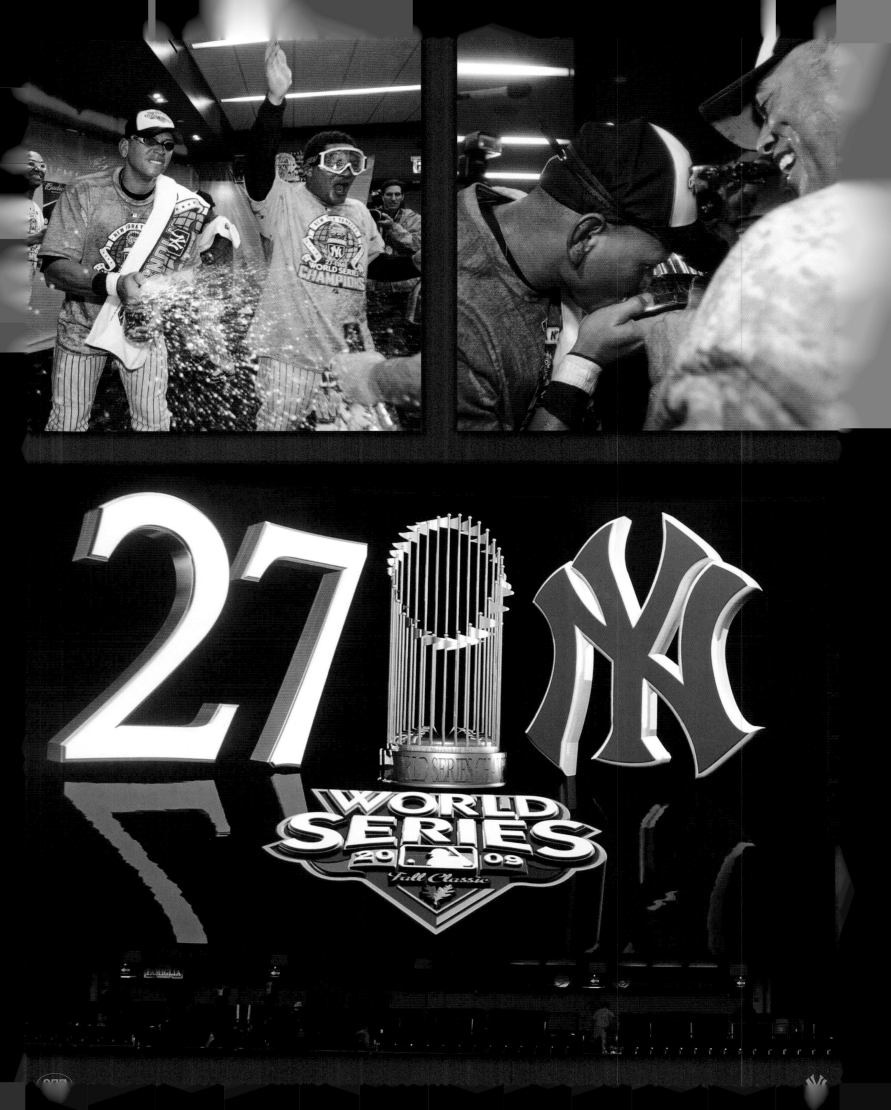

"First your goal is to win a championship, whether it's on or off the field. You figure out whatever your job is, whatever your task is. Do it to the best of your ability. Then help out your teammates along the way. If you do all those things, you have the right recipe for success."

— MARK TEIXEIRA

"I believe that the team really decided as a group that they wanted to do this — they wanted to win it for 'The Boss'. They had lived through seeing this amazing man and what he had done to put a championship team on the field, through the ups and downs of him, when he was screaming and yelling, and how proud he was of them at all moments. This group of guys appreciated that so much that they had fun, they worked hard, they worked together and they were there for each other. They went on to do it for 'The Boss'."

— Jenny Steinbrenner Swindall

THE BEAT GOES ON

"Our history has a foundation of tradition and of winning that has carried on decade after decade after decade. Dating back to the 1920's with "Murderer's Row" and all those great teams and the championships they won, then the guys playing in the 1950's who looked up to those past greats. And since the 1970's, we bang into the heads of these kids the moment they enter our system from the draft, that they're privileged to be playing for a team with such a rich history, and it carries on. It's something we instill in them — the rich history, the traditions, all the great players that have worn the pinstripes — and that they are privileged to wear them as well.

The Steinbrenner family is going to continue to do what we've been doing, which is expect excellence from our players the minute they walk in the door, whether they walk in as a free agent or they walk in as an eighteen year old kid that just got drafted. We're going to persevere, have courage, and do the best we can as long as we're involved, and because of that the tradition is going to continue, the winning is going to continue, and the fans are going to continue to come to the ball park and be proud to be associated with this organization."

— Hal Steinbrenner

Photography Credits

ALDS, ALCS and World Series Images
courtesy of the New York Yankees

Spring Training Images by Jerry Moores

Archival Images from Getty and Corbis

About the Author

Steve Yerrid has played and watched sports all of his life.
He has been a life-long New York Yankees fan and shared a
friendship with George Steinbrenner for over thirty years.
As Chairman of the Board for The Yerrid Foundation, he sup-
ports a number of charitable causes, particularly those seeking
to help children. As a trial lawyer, Mr. Yerrid has achieved great
success in a career dedicated to helping those who have been
wronged. He previously authored **When Justice Prevails,** a
non-fiction work dramatically detailing some of his most sig-
nificant courtroom trials, highlighted by inclusion of testimony
excerpts and the actual final summations made to the jury.
He continues to practice law and philanthropy, while living in
Tampa, Florida.

For more information on Steve Yerrid or The Yerrid Foundation,
go to www.yerridlaw.com

To 'The Boss'
and the entire Steinbrenner family –
This one's for you.
- STEVE YERRID